Dating God

and other bad ideas

NANCY SCHREYER

Foreword By Kris Vallotton

First Edition, 2022

ISBN: 979-8-9872162-0-0

Published by Corbin Publications
Ogden, Utah 84405

Corbin Publications is a division of Corbin Enterprises, LLC

Printed In the United States of America

DEDICATION

I dedicate this book to my incredible husband,
Shannon.

*Because you love me the way Christ loves the church, what others describe
as revelation seems like common sense to me. I don't have to dream or
imagine a marriage like God designed, or that godly, passionate husband
for which
every woman longs--I have you. You are such a
precious, undeserved gift to me from the Lord and
I am honored and blessed to spend
my life's adventure with you.
I adore you.*

To my children:
Caleb, Lydia and Ethan, Seth and Kimmy, and Anna.

*Don't ever settle for less than God's destiny for you.
Delight yourselves in Him and He will joyfully give
you the desires of your heart. Always see yourselves
through God's eyes. May our ceiling be your floor
and may your lives and your relationships
truly reflect Heaven on Earth.*

CONTENTS

ENDORSEMENTS

It is a delight for me to recommend Nancy's book. Nancy and Shannon have been wonderful, faithful friends for many years. In this book you will find good, Godly, sound advice and encouragement, aiding one to miss many pitfalls in relationships with others and your relationship with God. Your heart will be wonderfully warmed by the insights she shares. This book can be helpful in many aspects of one's life journey.

—BOBBY CONNER,
Prophet, founder of EaglesView Ministries
Author of multiple books including the *Shepherd's Rod.*

Nancy Schreyer writes the way she lives - honest, direct, and all-in. We love that about her and her book. In "Dating God and Other Bad Ideas" Nancy takes the reader on a journey into the hidden areas of the heart where unhealthy relational values and God concepts live, and exposes them to the light of truth. Yet, Nancy doesn't leave the reader exposed, but lays out a clear path that leads to a healthy, passionate and intimate relationship with the lover of our soul. Dating God and Other Bad Ideas is a must read for anyone looking for an upgrade.

—DAVID AND DEBORAH CRONE,
Senior leader of The Mission, Vacaville, Ca
Author of *Decisions That Define Us; The Power of Your Life Message; Declarations That Empower Us, and Prisoner of Hope.*

Nancy brings hilarious honesty and a loving urgency that will rekindle a passion for your first love. This book is like a truth grenade being tossed into the caverns of your soul that explosively shake up faulty mindsets and realign your heart to His. As you traverse these pages, you will rediscover the paths to union and limitless love.

—BRIAN ORME,
Founder of Anomali Ventures
and author of *The Ascended Life.*
www.iborme.com

ACKNOWLEDGEMENTS

To the women of God's Place:
You were the catalyst for this book.
You have stretched me and challenged me,
lovingly corrected and encouraged me.
You have given me hope and assurance that God is raising up a mighty
army of women to beautifully and powerfully complete the army of God.

I am proud and honored to serve with
you and be family with you.
You are amazing!

FOREWORD

Whether you are newly saved or have walked with the Lord for 50 years, Nancy Schreyer's book, *Dating God*, will awaken a divine romance with the Lover of Your Soul. This book is a step-by-step guidebook that will illuminate the path to true intimacy, and will inspire you to become a passionate lover of God. If you want to experience a deeper relationship with God, this book is for you.

KRIS VALLOTTON,
Senior Associate Leader, Bethel Church, Redding, CA
Co-Founder of Bethel School of Supernatural Ministry
Author of eleven books, including The Supernatural Ways
of Royalty and Fashioned to Reign.

INTRODUCTION

Me, a prostitute? An adulterer? Surely not! Perhaps not in the physical, yet throughout the Bible we see numerous examples of human relationships being representative of our spiritual relationship with God. There are examples of a father to his child, a mother to her baby, a king to his subjects, a master to his servants, and even those of a prostitute and an adulterous wife. Dating God is an exploration into the different relationships that can occur between a man and woman and how, many times, our relationship with God may mirror those same situations—good or bad. From a blind date and a budding romance, to the pit falls of dating around or even treating God as a "sugar daddy", we'll discover Jesus' heart for us and His desire to be in a passionate, fulfilling marriage with His bride.

In the Song of Songs we see a bride and groom deeply in love and longing for each other. In the fifth chapter of Ephesians Paul talks to the church about the balance in a healthy marriage, but he also explains that truly he is speaking about the mystery of the relationship between Christ and His body. Both of these examples speak not only about the corporate body of Christ but also us as individuals in an intimate, spiritual marriage to Jesus. Repeatedly we are shown Jesus' incredible love for us and His deep desire to be one with us, as a man and wife are one. God meant for marriage to be an earthly example, a reflection, of our relationship with Him.

My prayer is that you will open your heart and take an honest evaluation of your relationship with God—good or bad. Each situation may not apply to all of your life. It may just be one or two areas of your life that you have held back and not "committed to marriage." There will be times of laughing, crying, and even blushing and groaning with embarrassment at the realization of how we are truly treating the Lord.

But change can't come without revelation, repentance, and a new mindset, so take a deep breath and let's dive in. Your soul mate awaits!

Nancy

Section 1:
The Romance

Ah, romance! Nothing captures a woman's heart, at any age, like a love story. We are known for dragging the men in our lives to "chick flicks." It's a love test. They must pretend to enjoy and relate to even the most predictable, unrealistic story lines, while we sigh, clap, and wipe tears of both sorrow and joy from our mascara-stained faces. We are, by our God given nature, romantics. We believe in the fairy tale. We long for the fairy tale. Some of us spend our entire lives searching for the fairy tale. We dream of being swept off our feet, of our handsome prince fearlessly defending us no matter the foe. We imagine his words, sweet as honey, boldly and passionately declaring his undying love for us, a love that declares our beauty to only deepen with every wrinkle and stretch mark.

Yeah. . . seems ridiculous, I know. But guess what? God is a romantic. We get all that fairy tale stuff from Him. Jesus is Prince Charming---white horse and all! God loves a good love story, and He's written the very best one, because it really is based in perfect love. His is a love that is always faithful, passionate, and never-ending, that always sees us as beautiful, and never changes no matter how we fail. For so many of us that is almost impossible to believe. So we take our broken views of love and we impose them on our relationship with God. We then try to navigate a healthy relationship with Him based on lies our culture has told us.

But there's good news. God is out to romance you. In Old English, He is "wooing" you! Woowoo! He is deeply in love with you and it probably doesn't look like what you think it does. Jesus is after a bride. He has His eye on you to become His beautiful princess. You are about to begin the fairy tale….and it has an amazing ending.

Once upon time, in a place closer than you think, The Prince longed for His bride……

Jesus is not like any other man, and you will not be like any other woman after you encounter Him.

CHAPTER 1:
The Blind Date

"He can't be all that."

There are many ways in which God relates to us: as our father, brother, savior, judge, healer, comforter, provider---the list is endless. But as we look at the whole picture of a relationship with God, I think the best picture is one of a divine romance. That facet is the most intimate, most precious, most empowering relationship we can have with Him. We spend a lifetime seeking our soul mate, the one with whom we can spend the rest of our lives in true love. (Although men may grunt, shrug, and deny it's true, we ALL have that desire in us.) When we find that priceless treasure there is something that settles in our spirit, and then we have the wonderful adventure of spending the rest of our lives getting to know that treasure and fulfilling a greater purpose together than we could have had apart.

The desire to be in love begins at a very young age. The desire to be in love with God is created within us when God forms us in our mother's womb. We were created to be with Him, to know Him intimately. It is as though we have this God-shaped vacuum inside us, a longing that continually draws us towards Him. We may try any number of things to fill that void and stop the vacuum, but nothing completes it except Him. We were created for relationships. The only thing God said wasn't good about creation was man being alone. Many of us claim adamantly that we don't need anyone. We are independent, self-sufficient, and relationships are a crutch. I believe if we were honest with ourselves, we would admit we deeply want a relationship but are more afraid of being hurt than we are of being alone. None of us was created to live life alone, and none of us was created to be spiritually single.

When it comes to being romanced by God most of us come from one of three backgrounds:

One: We may have no idea at all who God is. As incredible as this may seem to many of us , there are people all around us who know Jesus only as a name. They literally know nothing about Him. What a wonderful opportunity for Jesus to be able to introduce Himself and for us to get to know Him for who He really is, without looking through tinted lenses that may not be accurate.

Two: We may have some knowledge of God, but all of our information may not be accurate. We may have heard stories or had some experiences we felt were orchestrated by Him, but because we don't really know Him or we have misinterpreted Him, or because others who talked about Him to us didn't really know Him, they misrepresented Him to us. If we judge Him by our experiences with the humans around us we are bound to misunderstand Him, to think He has the same faults and weaknesses as others, or that His love is conditional like everyone else's.

Let me give you an example of someone who thought she knew about God, but when she met Him face to face she found He was completely different and her life was radically changed.

John 4:4-29 NIV
⁴Now he had to go through Samaria. ⁵So he came to a town in Samaria called Sychar, near the plot of ground Jacob had given to his son Joseph. ⁶Jacob's well was there, and Jesus, tired as he was from the journey, sat down by the well. It was about the sixth hour.

⁷When a Samaritan woman came to draw water, Jesus said to her, "Will you give me a drink?" ⁸(His disciples had gone into the town to buy food.)

⁹The Samaritan woman said to him, "You are a Jew and I am a Samaritan woman. How can you ask me for a drink?" (For Jews do not associate with Samaritans.)

¹⁰Jesus answered her, "If you knew the gift of God and who it is that asks you for a drink, you would have asked him and he would have given you living water."

¹¹"Sir," the woman said, "you have nothing to draw with and the well is deep. Where can you get this living water? ¹²Are you greater than our father Jacob, who gave us the well and drank from it himself, as did also his sons and his flocks and herds?"

¹³Jesus answered, "Everyone who drinks this water will be thirsty again, ¹⁴but whoever drinks the water I give him will never thirst. Indeed, the water I give him will become in him a spring of water welling up to eternal life."

¹⁵The woman said to him, "Sir, give me this water so that I won't get thirsty and have to keep coming here to draw water."

¹⁶He told her, "Go, call your husband and come back."
¹⁷"I have no husband," she replied.

Jesus said to her, "You are right when you say you have no husband. ¹⁸The fact is, you have had five husbands, and the man you now have is not your husband. What you have just said is quite true."

¹⁹"Sir," the woman said, "I can see that you are a prophet. ²⁰Our fathers worshiped on this mountain, but you Jews claim that the place where we must worship is in Jerusalem."

²¹Jesus declared, "Believe me, woman, a time is coming when you will worship the Father neither on this mountain nor in Jerusalem.²²You Samaritans worship what you do not know; we worship what we do know, for salvation is from the Jews. ²³Yet a time is coming and has now come when the true worshipers will worship the Father in spirit and truth, for they are the kind of worshipers the Father seeks. ²⁴God is spirit, and his worshipers must worship in spirit and in truth."

²⁵The woman said, "I know that Messiah" (called Christ) "is coming. When he comes, he will explain everything to us."

²⁶Then Jesus declared, "I who speak to you am he."
The Disciples Rejoin Jesus

²⁷Just then his disciples returned and were surprised to find him talking with a woman. But no one asked, "What do you want?" or "Why are you talking

with her?"

²⁸Then, leaving her water jar, the woman went back to the town and said to the people, ²⁹"Come, see a man who told me everything I ever did. Could this be the Christ?"

Wow! God didn't look anything like she thought He would. Let's look at some of her misconceptions:

- She thought she could hide her life from Him.

- She thought if He knew about her life He would condemn her.

- She thought she could change the subject on Him.

- She thought He was just concerned about the rules, not the truth.

- She thought if He knew her He wouldn't love her.

- She thought He would treat her like every other man did.

- She thought He could offer her only the same thing any other man did.

Jesus is not like any other man and you will never be like any other woman after you encounter Him. You were designed by Him as an exquisitely unique creation, but until you are fulfilled and secure in His immeasurable love, you will spend your life futilely trying to please others by being someone you were never intended to be.

Three: We may have actually known God at one time, but then became offended with Him because we misunderstood Him or disagreed with Him. So we broke our covenant with Him or "divorced" Him and walked away. This is a difficult heart to deal with, because it has believed a lie and then been injured because of that lie. In order for there to be a restoration there must be an unveiling of the lie, an admission of believing it, forgiveness (on both sides of the relationship), and a deep healing to restore love and trust. It's a challenging process, but completely doable, and absolutely God's desire for us.

So, in a sense, the woman at the well got set up (by God) on a blind date! (Don't you love those parents who set their kids up?) There may be a few variations on this theme, but they're so similar. Jesus (our date) may talk to us Himself. He most likely won't do it face to face, but he may speak to us in our dreams, through gifts He sends us (life, provision, our family and friends…) or He may write us a note (hello---they call it the Bible!). He may go through a friend to set up the date. You know, he or she is always telling you, "I know the perfect guy you should meet. He's so awesome! Great sense of humor AND handsome! Talk about RICH! You have no idea!" and on and on…. Your first date with Him may be at a Bible study or some other church function, or you may have your first date with Him all on your own. Either way, my advice is: when God asks you out on a date, say yes!

Sadly, there can be difficult circumstances in our lives that propel us toward a date with God. We may be lonely, hurt, disappointed, confused, sick, dissatisfied, experiencing transition, or feeling purposeless. Although God doesn't ever harm us to draw us to Him, He will use the difficult things in our lives to turn our hearts toward Him so that we can have that intimate relationship with Him, and He can give us the amazing life He has planned for us. You may think you don't need God and would never want to spend your life with Him, but when things are hard, it's incredible how we're willing to broaden our options!

Sometimes, even when our date is with someone as amazing as Jesus, we can get cold feet. You know the saying, "If he sounds too good to be true, he probably is!"? Maybe in a previous relationship you thought you had found the perfect guy. You thought he would always love you and never leave you. You thought you would have a wonderful family with brilliant children and then grow old together while he swore you were more beautiful every day. But as soon as something or someone better came along, or as soon as life wasn't an easy street, he kicked you to the curb with the garbage. That'll put a bitter taste in your mouth. Maybe you think even if there were the perfect guy out there he would never want you. If any decent guy knew the things you had done, or the things that were done to you, or the kind of family you come from, he could never love you. You are so covered in shame and regret that you just can't believe anyone could care about you, and you're far too terrified to risk finding that out.

I have such good news for you! Jesus is that once-in-a-lifetime find! It's true! He will never leave you, trade you, abuse you, use you, fail you, or reject you! He is already passionately in love with you. And you don't have to worry about growing old or ugly because *"man looks on the outside, but God looks on the heart" (1 Samuel 16:7 NIV)* and He has already said, *"I find NO FLAW in you"*(Song of Songs 4:7)! He's not embarrassed by who you are or what you've done. He already knew all of that before He asked you out. The Bible says there is "no condemnation for those who are in Christ Jesus" (Romans 8:1). Woohoo! Jesus really is the perfect guy for you. His is literally a divine romance----worth the risk and worth the cost. He died just on the hope that you would go out with Him---top that!

If you don't know Jesus I'd love to set you two up! He is so easy to get to know. You can trust every word He tells you. Absolutely all of it is true. He's not exaggerating or feeding you a line. Maybe you thought you knew Him but throughout this chapter you're finding Him to be different than you thought. Believe the good. He is always good, all the time. It's easy to get into a real relationship with Him. All you have to do is tell Him you're sorry things aren't the way they are supposed to be in your life. Ask Him to show you the truth about any lies you have believed. Tell Him you're sorry for things you did that you knew were wrong or attitudes you've had toward Him or other people that were not loving or forgiving. He will forgive you immediately. He never holds a grudge. You don't have to play games with Him or wonder where you stand in the relationship. He always wants more. He's always ready to commit. He was madly in love with you before you ever even knew His name. What an awesome first date! It makes me believe in love at first sight!

CHAPTER 1:
Going Deeper

1. Our relationship with God can best be described as _____.

2. We are created with a _____ vacuum in us.

3. The only thing God said wasn't good about creation was _____.

4. None of us was created to be _____.

5. There are basically three different backgrounds when it comes to knowing God.

    a. _____

    b. _____

    c. _____

6.   What were some ways the woman at the well misunderstood Jesus?

_____

_____

_____

_____

_____

_____

7.   What are some ways Jesus may introduce Himself to us (set up a date)?

_____

_____

_____

_____

_____

_____

8.   What are some difficult circumstances that may propel us into accepting God's offer?

_____

_____

_____

_____

_____

_____

9.   Name three reasons we might get "cold feet" about giving God a chance.

a. _____

b. _____

c. _____

10. List three scriptures that say how God sees us.

a. _____

b. _____

c. _____

Notes / Thoughts / Prayers

_____
_____
_____
_____
_____
_____
_____
_____
_____
_____
_____
_____
_____
_____
_____
_____
_____
_____
_____
_____
_____
_____
_____
_____
_____
_____
_____
_____
_____
_____
_____

Being part of the body of Christ isn't about finding the perfect church. It's about growing together, challenging each other, encouraging each other, and most of all, loving each other through good and bad.

CHAPTER 2:
Dating Around

"I'm just not ready to settle down."

"So many men (or women if you're a guy), so little time!" Oh, the anguish of the ever-searching, never-satisfied Casanova! Like a modern day gun fighter, some of us move from relationship to relationship, victim to victim, putting the next notch of conquest on our belt. It's as though we see the opposite sex as a buffet of choices set before us that we are free to pick over and graze upon, leaving the unwanted choices discarded in a disgusting heap, to be wasted and thrown in the trash. Sound harsh? What if I tell you that we treat God that same way?

It's not new, nor are we the first ones to do so. Thousands of years ago the children of Israel made quite a habit of this behavior. No sooner had God delivered them miraculously from the hand of a cruel, pagan pharaoh than they became just a little too fidgety in the relationship. Let's see what transpired when they were asked to be faithful just for a brief period of time, without supervision:

Let's look at Exodus 32:1-8 NIV
1 When the people saw that Moses was so long in coming down from the mountain, they gathered around Aaron and said, "Come, make us gods who will go before us. As for this fellow Moses who brought us up out of Egypt, we

don't know what has happened to him."

2 Aaron answered them, "Take off the gold earrings that your wives, your sons and your daughters are wearing, and bring them to me." 3 So all the people took off their earrings and brought them to Aaron. 4 He took what they handed him and made it into an idol cast in the shape of a calf, fashioning it with a tool. Then they said, "These are your gods, O Israel, who brought you up out of Egypt."

5 When Aaron saw this, he built an altar in front of the calf and announced, "Tomorrow there will be a festival to the LORD." 6 So the next day the people rose early and sacrificed burnt offerings and presented fellowship offerings. Afterward they sat down to eat and drink and got up to indulge in revelry.

7 Then the LORD said to Moses, "Go down, because your people, whom you brought up out of Egypt, have become corrupt. 8 They have been quick to turn away from what I commanded them and have made themselves an idol cast in the shape of a calf. They have bowed down to it and sacrificed to it and have said, 'These are your gods, O Israel, who brought you up out of Egypt.'

We don't know exactly how long Moses was on the mountain, but apparently fewer than forty days. The fact that the people had time to complain to Aaron, gather all their jewelry, melt it down, craft an idol, make sacrifices to it, and then have a huge orgy, tells me that they gave up being faithful not long after Moses first left. Have you ever noticed how God's timeline and ours are vastly different? What we, in our immaturity and impatience, think of as an unbearable length of time is merely an instant to God.

I love how Aaron covered his tail when Moses came down to confront this whole mess. In verse 21 Moses asked Aaron, "What did these people do to you that you led them into such great sin?" Aaron's reply was classic:

Exodus 32:22-24 NIV
22 "Do not be angry, my lord," Aaron answered. "You know how prone these people are to evil. 23 They said to me, 'Make us gods who will go before us. As for this fellow Moses who brought us up out of Egypt, we don't know what has happened to him.' 24 So I told them, 'Whoever has any gold jewelry, take it off.' Then they gave me the gold, and I threw it into the fire, and out came this calf!"

I can just hear him, "It was the weirdest thing, Moses! You wouldn't believe it unless you had seen it! You know these people are just really messed up and I tried to set them straight. They were all worried about you and thought you had been killed by wild animals. (Forget the fact that they just saw God put ten plagues on their enemies and then there was that little 'walking through the sea on dry land' miracle. I can see why they would be worried about poor little Moses' safety.) I was just trying to calm them down, keep their minds off all the worrying. So I told them to gather all their gold—you know, it's just all those reminders of Egypt-- and when I threw it in the fire this calf jumped out! It was so wild!"

Nice try, Aaron.

Oh, but we give just as ridiculous excuses for trying other gods, don't we?

"I've been giving faithfully for six months, but I'm still in huge debt! I think I'm going to take my tithe and put it toward my debt."

"They say God still heals people, but I've had people pray and my pain is still unbearable. I bought some crystals, and I signed up for some sessions with a hypnotist. I think God can use a lot of different methods."

"I turned my life over to God because I'm so tired of the loneliness and depression, but I've waited and waited and He still hasn't brought me a spouse, so I went ahead and put a profile on an online dating service and broadened my criteria. I want someone who's a Christian, but I think they'll commit to God once we start dating. God helps those who help themselves, right?"

Sadly, when God doesn't jump through the right hoop, or our relationship with Him doesn't turn out to be the dream date, we move on. Maybe He just wasn't Mr. Right (because what we really wanted was Mr. Right Now). Jesus might be fine for someone else, but He's just not my type.

The Israelites weren't very good at committing to their relationship with God over the long haul. If Jehovah didn't seem to scratch their itch, they just turned to the next god. They went through periods where they worshiped multiple gods, from multiple religions, right along side the True God.

Judges 2:12,13 NIV
12 They forsook the LORD, the God of their fathers, who had brought them out of Egypt. They followed and worshiped various gods of the peoples around them. They provoked the LORD to anger 13 because they forsook him and served Baal and the Ashtoreths.

They saw no conflict of interest until God allowed disaster to fall on them just to remind them about that "Thou shalt have no other gods before me" rule. Then there would be wailing, repenting, and promising God that He was the only one for them (at least until they got out of trouble). Sound familiar?

Sometimes even as believers we do the same thing with the body of Christ. We go from church to church, never finding the perfect match. We may leave one because it just wasn't exciting enough, or we weren't being "fed." Maybe we just didn't feel important enough or couldn't make connections. Or maybe the church seemed incredible, until that first conflict when we found out (much to our surprise) that it was made up of imperfect humans (including the pastor)! Rather than work through the situation, we just left and went to look for a "safe" church where we wouldn't get hurt (or be expected to resolve conflicts). Notice that none of these issues even pertain to basic doctrines of Christianity? Here's a news flash: there is no perfect match when it comes to finding a church. Churches are led by, and filled with, people. Being part of the body of Christ isn't about finding the perfect church. It's about growing together, challenging each other, encouraging each other, and most of all, loving each other through good and bad.

In other cases, we may see God as this colossal "kill-joy" with whom a relationship could be nothing but a monotonous life of somber church services and self-denial. Nothing could be farther from the life Jesus has promised us. Jesus gave His very life so we could have life "to the full" (John 10:10 NIV). The Message puts it this way:

John 10:10 The Message
*10 I came so they can have real and eternal life, more and better life than they
ever dreamed of.*

A life sold out to Christ is a life of unimaginable joy and adventure (Romans 14:7). It is not always easy, but I assure you it is never boring. The God of the Bible is described as "fiery" (Ezekiel 22), "strong and loving" (Psalm 62:11&12), "jealous" (Exodus 34:14), and a God who "rejoices over you with singing" (Zephaniah 3:17)! "Boring" is never mentioned. God's heart is not to ruin your life with a list of rules. He has a destiny planned for you beyond your wildest dreams.

I am aware that there are people who choose, for perfectly healthy reasons, to remain single all of their lives. I certainly don't believe that everyone is meant to be married, nor am I campaigning for arranged marriages or an end to dating. I am referring to those who constantly move from one relationship to the next, never satisfied, always looking for the next relationship as soon as the current one becomes uncomfortable.

The true motivation behind this behavior is largely self-protective and fear-based. It's all about finding what you think will make you happy: the excitement, the flattery, the attention, or even avoiding commitment due to the fear of being controlled or being stuck in a less than perfect situation. It really has no concern for others. It is a constant cycle of frustration and disappointment.

You will never find fulfillment endlessly dating around. You will never find that life-long love by constantly moving from one relationship to another. Things of great worth come from a long term investment or process. A diamond isn't formed overnight, crops don't grow effortlessly and instantly, one doesn't learn all she or he needs to know in one day of school, and confident, well-balanced children aren't created with a weekend visit or an annual birthday card from the absentee parent. Whether it be in a human relationship or your relationship with God, true satisfaction can only come by making a lifetime commitment, heart and soul, to someone with the same vision, passion, and core values as you. That can't happen with multiple partners or a short term relationship. Matthew 22:37 clearly states that we are to "Love the Lord your God with all your heart, with all your mind, and with all your soul."

The excitement of true love is spending your life pouring into someone else's dreams while they pour into yours. It's about spending a lifetime getting to know someone intimately on every level, with the assurance that no matter what is found, the commitment never waivers. A covenant relationship with Jesus Christ is all this and much more. The value and depth of our romance with Him grows with every day we commit to Him, every difficulty we trust Him through, every new, wonderful facet of Him we uncover, and every part of ourselves we surrender. Being faithful in a covenant is not always easy, it is not always understandable or explainable, it is not always what we feel like doing, but it is always worth it and is the only thing that will fulfill the desire of our heart.

CHAPTER 2:
Going Deeper

1. What did the Israelites do that ticked God off so badly in Exodus Chapter 32?

    _____

    _____

    _____

    _____

    _____

2. What was their excuse?

    _____

    _____

    _____

    _____

    _____

3. Give three excuses you may give to "date around" on God.

    a. _____

    b. _____

    c. _____

4. List one or more areas of your life in which you have dated "other gods."

    _____

    _____

    _____

    _____

    _____

    _____

    _____

5. What is really the core motivation for "dating around" (on God or people)?

    _____

    _____

    _____

    _____

    _____

    _____

6. What are some reasons people date around on churches?

    _____

    _____

    _____

    _____

    _____

    _____

    _____

7.   What is necessary for "true love" to occur?

_____

_____

_____

_____

_____

_____

Reflection:

Please take time to examine your heart and talk to the Lord. Let Holy Spirit show you any ways in which you may be "dating around" on God. His heart is passionate for you and He longs to have you love Him the way He loves you. He is a jealous God because He has paid such a high price for you — the death of His Son. If you will make the commitment to Him, it will absolutely be one you will never regret.

Notes/ Thoughts/ Prayers

_____

_____

_____

_____

_____

_____

_____

_____

_____

_____

_____

_____

_____

_____

_____

God longs to be your husband,
not your boyfriend.

CHAPTER 3:

Going Steady

"We got a good thing going

why complicate it?"

Going steady with God is, in many cases, the next step in the relationship. It is definitely an improvement over the "dating around" stage. It shows a maturing on our part in many ways. Hopefully, it means we have moved past the "it's all about me" stage. We're moving toward true commitment, toward at least some level of intimacy. There are a lot of perks that come with going steady. Let's take a look at a few and then we'll look at some of the drawbacks.

Perk #1: At least you have a relationship.

You have an answer to that awkward, "Are you seeing anybody?" question. In the church world that's translated as "Where ya goin' to church now?" It's just too embarrassing to admit we're not involved with anyone (or should I say any "body"?). You're past the frustration and confusion of dating around and feel like things are beginning to make sense. You have at least a basic commitment and an expectation of reasonable faithfulness from both parties. You're wondering if this could be "the one" with whom you'll spend your life ? Somehow we just feel like we have our lives more together if we have a relationship going on. Our lives have more worth, more focus. We have more of a purpose. We have a connection with someone. We're important to someone.

Perk #2: You have someone to hang out with.

Gee, what do you do with your life when you don't have a significant other? What a bummer to go to the movies by yourself, or that awkward sitting at a restaurant by yourself with everyone staring at you. Who do you take with you to all those torturous office parties and weddings? Who do you call when you get that promotion or have a fight with the boss? Going steady solves all those problems in the natural, and going steady with God (and His church) solves a lot of it, too. Many people try to substitute going steady with the church for an intimate marriage to God. Look at the benefits: You have all your church friends to hang out with (and since you all know you're supposed to behave the activities are pretty safe). There's always something to do involving the church, whether it's recreational or work related. It's pretty easy to get really involved so you can ignore that emptiness you feel when you get home at night. You have a church family that cares how your week went and will pray for you during hard times, so if there's something really tough, you can definitely call.

Perk #3: You really like the way He makes you feel.

Whether it's physical or emotional, there's just a lot to be said about how having a "steady" makes us feel. From the way we smile when we think about him, to the way our heart can pound when he touches us, are all wonderful parts of going steady. We can certainly have the same thrill from God. We come into a church service and feel His presence. Sometimes it's so gentle and sweet, while other times we may feel completely overwhelmed and find ourselves weeping. In the natural it's a wonderful feeling to have someone care about how you feel, to have someone go out of his or her way to take care of you, or take the time to do special things for you. When we begin to "go steady" with God we can be amazed by the depth of His love for us and the many ways He takes care of us. As He meets different needs in our lives and blesses us, we may find ourselves thinking how wonderful it is that we found such a great guy with whom to share our lives!

Great perks and a definite improvement over dating around! Problem is: you're still not married. In spite of all the benefits, going steady still has undeniable drawbacks. Let's check out some of those:

Drawback #1: The commitment only goes so far.

Although there is certainly far more commitment involved in going steady than in dating around, it's still not a permanent relationship. You're still deciding if this is who you want. You're committed to him –at least while you're dating him. But the reality is that it may not last, and you certainly haven't given your life to him. In your mind you're still looking, open to other options. The same is true when you just "go steady" with God. You may be somewhat committed, but you've certainly not given Him your life. At this stage of the game that would seem unreasonable, too much to ask. In your mind and heart you are still looking to see if there is something or someone else that catches your eye. You're still not fully convinced Jesus is the one with whom you want to spend your life. Could there be someone better? Someone more exciting? More beautiful? Richer? Never. Will He love you the rest of your life? Can you really be happy with Him? Will you be fulfilled? Always.

Drawback #2: Being in a steady relationship doesn't necessarily mean being in love.

Although the thrill of it can be exciting and the security of it can be comfortable, going steady isn't an assurance of being in love. Many times the relationship is growing and it may progress to that point, but sadly, many people find themselves going steady just to keep from being alone. There is no deepening of the relationship, no stronger commitment—they simply are together because they don't see any better option out there. There are endless reasons why people get in, and stay in, relationships like this— none of them healthy, productive, or fulfilling. Yet everyone truly longs for the same thing—to be deeply and passionately in love. It is a desire God Himself has put in us—to love and be loved. Any difficulty in a relationship can be overcome if there is the love, commitment, and determination to follow God's guidelines to work through the problem. But without love as the motivation, there will never be the determination to see it through. Truly being in love does not insure a perfect, problem-free world, but traveling through life with someone you love is a journey of challenge, growth, laughter, and fulfillment.

God longs to get past "going steady" with us. Some of us stay in a quasi-relationship with God because we're comfortable there. We like all the perks of being with Him, but in our hearts we haven't made the full commitment. We are still open to other options, still looking around. We don't want to mess up what we have, but we'd leave Him if we felt like something better came along. We would say we are committed, but if more were required of us than that with which we were comfortable, we would break off the relationship because it was unreasonable. Sound extreme? Would you literally die for Christ? Would you give Him all your money? If you were sick the rest of your life would you still believe He is good? What if you lost one of your children or other family members? Would you still believe Him to be wonderful and merciful? What if He asked you to give up your job and home because He wanted you somewhere else? What if He asked you to give up some of your friends because they were coming between the two of you? If you think any of these would be asking too much, then you're still going steady.

Remember the wedding vows "For richer, for poorer, in sickness and in health, 'til death do you part"? Marriage is a whole different ballgame from going steady. But you will never receive from going steady what you will from being married. God longs to be your husband, not your boyfriend.

Drawback #3: You can be only so intimate.

Society today has crossed so many of the God-given boundaries of intimacy. It seems the pendulum has swung from one extreme to the other — neither extreme being biblical. One side of the pendulum said intimacy, physical or emotional, was inappropriate. Propriety demanded that intimacy be viewed as a necessary evil, that physical and emotional passion were not dignified or proper, especially for believers. Physical intimacy was meant only for propagation, strictly a practical purpose, and emotional passion was seen as a lack of control, an evil weakness, not admirable among respectable persons.

Even a short amount of time spent reading the Bible will shatter these beliefs. You will not find a more passionate love story, physically or emotionally, than the Song of Songs. I'm reminded of my husband's Bible college professor who taught Old Testament. He would joke that his wife always knew when the curriculum had arrived on the Song of Songs because he became a man with a renewed focus! Yet it is not only an intimate account of an earthly relationship, but also a reflection of Jesus' passion and desire to be with us as His bride. Read through 1 and 2 Samuel and the Psalms to see how emotional David was about worshipping his God. Study what the original Hebrew words for "praise" mean. Obviously, God is passionate! He created intimacy, both physical and emotional. And He also created the environment in which they flourish.

The other side of pendulum has understood intimacy and passion to be normal, healthy desires, but it has not understood that they can be so only in a setting blessed by God. Sex was totally God's idea. So was the incredible pleasure that comes with it! That's a shocker to a lot of people. But sex is meant not only for the creation of children or for the physical pleasure of it. Sex is a physical, even prophetic, symbol of what is going on spiritually between two people. They become one. There is a submitting to one another, a giving of one's self to the other. They are no longer two separate entities but now they complement each other to become one amazing unit. And out of that union comes new life, a new creation that is a blending of the two—a creation that would not have been possible without that sacred intimacy.

But that union is truly successful only within the covenant—the total commitment—of marriage. Sex outside of that bond is cheapened. The physical act cannot hold value as a spiritual act without the covenant. It is devalued to shallow pleasure, to a using of each other, and it will leave a permanent scar when the two are parted (1 Corinthians 6:16,17). Sex outside of marriage is not true intimacy, and sex, even inside of marriage, without the giving of one's self spiritually to the other, is reduced to the same thing.

Intimacy is meant to occur in a marriage on every level, not just physically. A fulfilling marriage has intellectual, emotional, and spiritual intimacy as well. None of that can happen when you go steady. You just don't have the commitment to each other for it to occur. There's no depth, no root—the relationship can't grow that deeply and when the sun scorches down on it, it will die.

God longs to be intimate with us on every level. He is not a God who just wants to sit and watch from a distance. He has completely given Himself to us, with no promise of anything in return. He wants to know all of you. He strongly desires you to trust Him completely and surrender all your being to Him. Only then can there be that amazing union between the two of you, and only then will such incredible new life be birthed in you. You will be astonished at the new plans, purposes, and dreams to which you will give birth and at how quickly His kingdom will grow.

Drawback #4: There is no real security.

As we've already established, there is a certain level of commitment while going steady, but it is not without its limits. Therefore, our level of security within that relationship has its limits also. Security comes with ownership. Let me explain. If you rent your home, you have a place to live, but it's not really yours. You aren't free to make whatever changes you want. You must always ask the owner's permission. If you keep up with your rental payments everything should be fine, but there is always the possibility that the owner will change his mind and make you move. You don't really have any control over your situation, because the house does not belong to you. If you have a mortgage on your house, it's better than renting. You have the freedom to make whatever changes you would like to your house; you answer to no one. Much like renting, as long as you keep up on your mortgage payments you will have a home in which to live, and you are making progress toward truly owning the home. The problem is, you still don't fully own it. If your circumstances take a bad turn you could still lose your home. You are never really secure until you fully own it.

Going steady has the same problem. There is a level of security, but because you have not given "ownership" of yourselves to each other, there's always the chance that the relationship will end. There is the idea that you don't really owe that person anything, because after all, they don't "own" you. Ownership in a marriage is not a negative thing. It is a mutual desire to fully give yourselves to each other.

1 Corinthians 7:4 NIV
4 The wife's body does not belong to her alone but also to her husband. In the same way, the husband's body does not belong to him alone but also to his wife.

This is not only true of each other's body, but also every aspect of each other's life. The Bible speaks of marriage as being a reflection of what our relationship with Christ should be.

Ephesians 5:25-33 NIV
25 Husbands, love your wives, just as Christ loved the church and gave himself up for her 26 to make her holy, cleansing her by the washing with water through the word, 27 and to present her to Himself as a radiant church, without stain or wrinkle or any other blemish, but holy and blameless. 28 In this same way, husbands ought to love their wives as their own bodies. He who loves his wife loves himself. 29 After all, no one ever hated his own body, but he feeds and cares for it, just as Christ does the church — 30 for we are members of His body. 31 "For this reason a man will leave his father and mother and be united to his wife, and the two will become one flesh." 32 This is a profound mystery — but I am talking about Christ and the church. 33 However, each one of you also must love his wife as he loves himself, and the wife must respect her husband.

Security in a marriage comes from a mutual "ownership" of each other--not a controlling, manipulative ownership that serves only one person's needs, but a loving, giving of oneself gladly for the other. It's not a matter of being in control of each other, but a matter of being responsible to care for and love each other. In that relationship there is complete security, because no circumstance will change that — good or bad.

God has given us that absolute security. He completely gave Himself to us before we even agreed to reciprocate. Nothing nor anyone can change that.

Romans 8:35-39
35 Who shall separate us from the love of Christ? Shall trouble or hardship or persecution or famine or nakedness or danger or sword? 36 As it is written:

"For your sake we face death all day long;

we are considered as sheep to be slaughtered."
37 No, in all these things we are more than conquerors through him who loved
us. 38 For I am convinced that neither death nor life, neither angels nor demons,
neither the present nor the future, nor any powers, 39 neither height nor depth,
nor anything else in all creation, will be able to separate us from the love of God
that is in Christ Jesus our Lord.
Now <u>that's</u> security!

Going steady with God may be an improvement over dating around, but it will never be the relationship for which you really long. Come on, quit looking for Mr. Right. You already found Him. Jump in! Get serious! You will have a more amazing life than you ever dreamed!

CHAPTER 3:
Going Deeper

List three perks to going steady:

Perk # 1

_____

_____

_____

_____

Perk # 2

_____

_____

_____

_____

Perk # 3

_____
_____
_____
_____

List four drawbacks to going steady:

Drawback # 1

_____
_____
_____
_____

Drawback # 2

_____
_____
_____
_____

Drawback # 3

_____
_____
_____
_____

Drawback # 4

_____
_____
_____
_____

What does "ownership" as discussed in this chapter look like?

_____

_____

_____

_____

What thoughts or beliefs might keep someone from moving forward from "going steady" to getting married in the spiritual sense?

_____

_____

_____

_____

Name some reasons why we can trust Jesus to not only be our "steady," but our husband.

_____

_____

_____

_____

Notes / Thoughts / Prayers

_____

_____

_____

_____

_____

_____

_____

_____

_____

_____

Healthy, loving relationships are not about what we can get out of them but what we can pour into them.

CHAPTER 4:
The Engagement

"You're not married 'til you're married."

Wow! There just isn't a much more thrilling day than the day he pops "The Question"! So much excitement, so much anticipation, so many nerves, and most of all—how about that rock? Being engaged is a whole different world from going steady. In your heart and mind, you've decided he is the one.

If going steady had a somewhat stabilizing effect on your life, then being engaged does even more so. You are definitely feeling focused, settling in on this major part of your life. What you thought to be the biggest question of your life is now answered, at least in your head.

Now all the planning begins. It takes a lot of preparation to spend your lives together. There are financial obligations to figure out, perhaps educational pursuits to finish, legal requirements, vocational moves to make, details about where to live, getting to know each other's family, premarital counseling, all the plans involved in the wedding itself, including but not limited to bridesmaids, groomsmen, candle lighters, flower girl, ring bearer, pictures, colors, church reservation, flowers, music, the dress, the tuxes, the rings, the cake, invitations, the programs, servers, ushers, plans for the honeymoon, bridal showers, keeping your mother happy (and his!), and registering for the all-important china pattern! Whew! One could feel the G-force increasing as we read through the list!

There is so much involved with thinking about and planning to get married that sometimes we forget the most important part—the relationship! The focus is all around the event, the fairy tale, the romance, but many times I'm afraid we love the drama, the attention, and the excitement more than we love the person.

Embarrassingly, we do the same thing with Jesus. Some of us have become "engaged" to Christ, even to His church in a sense. We've met, fallen in love, decided this is with whom we want to spend the rest of our life. We've settled in, perhaps even signed up for membership with a church. We're getting to know each other well, spending lots of time with His family and Him. We already see ourselves as part of the family; we feel like we're home. Maybe we even have the ring (or in this case the cross or the fish). We wear it proudly, showing it off to our friends as a symbol of our relationship. When people see it, they should know that you're His; after all, you wouldn't wear His jewelry if you didn't have a real commitment---would you?

My father was one of the wisest men I have ever known, and he had a saying, "You're not married 'til you're married." I know, it seems he had a keen sense of the obvious, but you'd be amazed at how many people don't get that. Talk to any pregnant teenager whose boyfriend told her they'd be together forever, but now she hasn't heard from him since he heard the news. Have you ever met a girl whose livelihood was collecting engagement rings? Talk to any of the men that planned their lives with her. Even under the best of circumstances engagements can end, and all the planning, all of the dreams of growing old together, end.

Even legally, you're not married 'til you're married. You don't get any of the legal benefits of being married until you have that legal piece of paper signed. You can't take his name until you have fully made that commitment, both spiritually and legally. Truthfully, it is not even completely binding until a physical union has occurred. Both the Bible and the court system agree that you're not "one" until that happens. That should give you a reality check on the serious commitment sex is and why it was never meant to occur outside of marriage. It is a legal, physical, and spiritual bond that is not easily broken.

I realize that currently, in our society, there is a push to give the benefits of a holy covenant to those who are not in one. Those who desire benefits without covenant want to present those against this as selfish, small minded, and intolerant. And yet truth is truth. God designed marriage. He designed covenant. He designed both because He is a giving God who understands that healthy, loving relationships are not about what we can get out of them, but what we can pour into them. He has always been the one to love first, give first, sacrifice first. To demand rights and benefits when one is not willing to commit or one wants to live in an ungodly situation, but have God's blessing on it, is the height of deceit. We lie to ourselves and others, and in the end the hollow, heartbreaking truth of false relationships will always leave us alone by those whose goal was never to love, but to use.

So, follow my lead here—spiritually it is also true: "You're not married 'til you're married." You can wear the jewelry, have the fish on your car, wear the t-shirt, and hang out with the family, but if you haven't made a lifetime commitment, if you don't have that personal, intimate relationship with Jesus Christ—you're not married! Engagement is fun and exciting, but it's still not a marriage.

Let's look at some of the benefits you don't get when you're just engaged:

1. True intimacy.

We talked about this in the last chapter somewhat, but as with "going steady," you can be only so intimate when you're engaged. You aren't "one" in every sense. Sex when you're just engaged is tainted; it can't bring the same fulfillment as sex inside of marriage. That excitement, that high from being touched by someone to whom you have no commitment is a false high. We do that with God. We want Him to touch us, we want the warm fuzzies, "Jesus bumps", or supernatural encounter, but when He asks for our lives we're not ready to give them. The Bible tells of those who will come before Him on judgment day bragging about all the deeds they have done and God will send them away because He never "knew" them. They had talked and talked about their relationship with Jesus, but there was no real intimacy, no true submitting of their lives to Him, no real relationship—it was all talk. Jesus asked His Father to make us "one" the way He and the Father are "one"—completely, body, mind, and soul (John 17:11). He said that while He was still in a human body so that we could understand that it's possible.

2. You do not have his name.

In an earthly relationship and in our relationship with God this is the same principle. In the great majority of cultures, when you are not married you cannot legally use that person's name. All the rights and privileges that go with that name are not yours. You do not have access to any asset belonging to that person, be it finances, real estate, investments, etc. You are also not included under his healthcare or insurance. You cannot sign documents as his wife, and you cannot use his name with any authority, because it's not your name.

You can take that into a spiritual reality also. When you are not in that covenant relationship with God, when you're not "married" yet, you do not have His name. Revelation 2 talks about God giving us a new name. All through the Bible you can see the power in a name, especially the name of Jesus. We'll get into that a lot deeper when we discuss the marriage, but suffice it to say now, without having His name, you basically have no rights in the kingdom. You don't have access to kingdom finances, divine health, supernatural healing, protection, or blessing. God is so good that at times He will be gracious to you and give you these things to an extent, but you don't have a right to them as you would if you carried His name.

3. Your children do not have his name.

Any child born out of wedlock is illegitimate. My heart is not to condemn anyone who has had a child out of wedlock, but the fact is, that was not God's plan. We understand that God can redeem any situation, and for every human born He has a wonderful destiny and purpose, regardless of the circumstances of his or her conception, but God's plan is for every child to be born into the stability, support, discipline, and protection of a father and mother and for that child to have the full blessing of a son or daughter. The same is true spiritually. When we try to "birth" our own ideas, plans, ministries, dreams, outside of an intimate relationship with Christ, out from under the covering and protection of the Father, they are illegitimate "children." They are not birthed inside a covenant and they do not carry the Father's name or His blessing. They are doomed to frustration and failure because they don't have the blessing of His covering, favor, authority, and inheritance.

4. Ownership.

We talked briefly about this in the last chapter, but even in an engagement, there is no permanent ownership. You can make all the plans and promises in the world, but an engagement still doesn't require any legal action to end it. It's not a binding contract. It's an agreement, not a covenant. Either party can walk away by just saying they want to end it. That's far short of marriage. 1 Corinthians 6:20 says that when we make that covenant with God we have been "bought with a price." That price was the highest price that's ever been paid for anything. You are that precious to Him.

A healthy engagement is a wonderful time, a time in which the bride-to-be is consumed with love for her groom. Her focus is on the day when they can finally be together, finally become one. If you are in that stage with Jesus today, that's awesome! You need to understand that when it comes to marrying Jesus, you don't need to work yourself silly to have everything perfect before you marry Him. You don't need to fret over the future—He's got it all worked out. (See Jeremiah 29:11.) You don't need to lose weight to fit into that dress—He already sees you as flawless through His blood (Song of Songs 5:3). You don't need to worry about where you will live—He already has a place prepared for you (John 14:2). Jesus' desire is to marry you TODAY--no more planning, no more preparation, no more waiting. Walk down that aisle and make the commitment today!

CHAPTER 4:
Going Deeper

1.   Engagement can be such an exciting time. What can be the danger though, in the midst of all the excitement?

   _____

   _____

   _____

   _____

   _____

   _____

2.   What are some signs of being in the "engagement" stage?

   _____

   _____

   _____

_____
_____
_____

3.   Slogan for the chapter:

_____
_____
_____
_____
_____
_____

4.   Benefits you don't get while you are engaged:

_____
_____
_____
_____
_____
_____

5.   List some scriptures concerning God's plans for you:

_____
_____
_____
_____
_____
_____

Notes / Thoughts / Prayer

_____
_____
_____

CHAPTER 4: THE ENGAGEMENT

Section 2:
Perversions In The Relationship

Just as there are many wonderful relationships, there are also those that are equally as horrible. Sadly, this can be as true in our spiritual relationship to Jesus Christ as it is can be in our human relationships. Our marriage on this earth is to be a mirror of the relationship Christ longs to have with us, the perfect marriage He designed before we were even created. Unfortunately, many of us have difficulty grasping what that perfect relationship is or how it should function. We may have had tragic events happen to us, whether it be abuse, abandonment, betrayal, or any other unthinkable situation. It may have not been an event or series of events but simply a mindset taught to us from the time we were young, a set of beliefs that twisted the true meaning of love and marriage, so much so that we can't distinguish those lies from the truth. Either case can be incredibly damaging and keep us from ever having the love for which we have always longed and dreamed.

In this section we will discover how the perversions and misconceptions we carry into our earthly relationships can carry over into our relationship with Jesus. There will be humorous comparisons and others that are pretty gritty, but as in all things, only the truth will set you free. These truths may make you laugh at yourself one minute and be offended at the implication the next. You may find that you have these misperceptions and perversions in only certain areas of your relationships. Let Holy Spirit show those to you and bring health to those specific areas. Let your mind be open and your heart soft and pliable. Look at yourself and your marriage to Him through His eyes and His perfect love.

We steal His heart by giving ours
fully to Him.

CHAPTER 5:

A Sugar Daddy For A Trophy Wife

"He gives me everything I want and I make Him look good!"

It always amazes me how we can see the atrocity of someone else's behavior but never see that same characteristic in ourselves. We can see their selfishness, laziness, arrogance, insecurity, or dishonesty but we are blind to our own weaknesses in those same areas. We have that same uncanny ability when it comes to relationships. We can analyze any other relationship, diagnose the problem, and give, what in our mind is, priceless wisdom, all the while never seeing the very same problem in our own.

It is so easy for us to spot a "user." You know, the person who is in the relationship only for what he or she can get out of it? There are an equal number of male and female offenders in this category, but for the flow of the story, let's make this one female. I like to call it the "Sugar Daddy Syndrome." We've all seen the typical scenario: she's young and beautiful (usually without a penny to her name), he's older (but apparently not wiser) and very well-to-do. They work out an usually unspoken agreement that they see as mutually beneficial to one another. He gets a gorgeous "Trophy Wife" to hang on his arm, thus insuring all those around him that he is still young, virile, and desirable, and she gets every material thing her little heart desires so she never has to work or think, just look good.

Now some of us, hopefully jokingly, would love to have such an arrangement! After all, they're consenting adults right? Isn't a relationship about meeting each other's needs? They're each getting what they want and they both understand the rules of the game, so what's the problem?

Oh, where to begin! Let's look at what a healthy relationship should truly do for a person. True, part of a relationship is about meeting each other's needs—focus on the word "needs." The needs met in a relationship should first of all be legitimate needs, not wants. Secondly, they should be normal, healthy needs, not twisted, dysfunctional needs. Is the "need" to have every material desire given to you with no effort on your part, a healthy, legitimate need? In the long run, does having that need met improve you as a person? Does it deepen your character? Call you into greater maturity? Challenge you into being someone who will contribute to improving the lives of others and society in general? Uh. . . no.

What does having that "need" as the motivation in your relationship do for the other person? What does it say about the depth of your love for him? Of all the wedding vows (for richer, for poorer, in sickness and in health, for better or for worse), you agreed to only one-third of them. Your love is as deep as his bank account. You have no value for him as a person. He could be an ATM for all you care. What if he had the same criteria for loving you? You would be flat out of luck! Doesn't really qualify for true love, does it? Oh, a woman like that is just so shallow! We would never be like that, would we?

What about him? Is he innocent here? Oh, I think not. What does this relationship say about his true opinion of her? Does he love her mind? Her compassion for others? Her sense of humor? Her deep moral convictions? Okay, quit laughing. They were all rhetorical questions. Upon first glance, we may think his motivation is that he just wants her body (and yes, that would be a requirement), but upon further study we would find that it is more about his ego than her body. If he just wanted a body he could go to a prostitute. This isn't about that. She's a Barbie doll. You dress her up, take her with you, and show her off to your friends, who in turn are supposed to be insanely jealous and think you must really be amazing to have gotten such a prize. It's a whole different motivation.

In both people, the "needs" that are being met are purely selfish and rooted in deep brokenness in each person's heart. They do nothing positive for either party. There is no health or personal growth involved on either side. There is no love involved on either side. It is purely a matter of using each other. It is such a distortion of what God designed a relationship to be, especially a marriage. Marriage is meant to be a giving of one's self to the other, having a heart that desires to see the other person come to his or her full potential in every area. Marriage is meant to reflect the kind of love Jesus had for us when He gave everything for us, having no guarantee of anything in return.

Even if we would never consider getting involved in such a relationship on a human level, we can fall into this same mindset when it comes to our relationship with God. We may get involved with God because we think He's the answer to all our problems, and truly He is, but the way He answers is not always the quick fix for which we are looking. Some of us come into this relationship thinking that since we have found the Creator of the Universe, the Owner of All Things, He will be an endless supply of financial and material wealth, and we will never have another financial or material need. Even in other areas we expect never to have another problem. We think we'll never be sick again, and that no one we love will be sick or die "before their time." We think we'll get every promotion, or even get to quit our job, our children will be perfect, and our husband will cook dinner from now on (and wash the dishes, of course).

I actually had a discussion with a lady once that basically went like this:

Me: Wow! How have you been? I haven't seen you for quite a while.

She: Oh, I've been living in Florida for the last year just seeking God and waiting for Him to tell me what He wants me to do next.

Me: That's incredible! It's wonderful that you have the financial means to do that.

She: Oh, I don't. I've had to file bankruptcy because God just wouldn't let me get a job; He told me just to wait on Him.

Me: How did you live?

She: Oh, I've been living with my brother's family. That's the only way I would have made it.

That scenario may sound incredibly spiritual but it goes against what the Bible says in 2 Thesselonians 3:10 that if someone is unwilling to work then they shouldn't get to eat. And the Bible speaks in numerous places about paying back one's debt. I believe this woman thought she had a noble quest, but she didn't understand the flaws in her thinking.

God is not your Sugar Daddy. He is not here to baby you and give you everything you want. He will take care of your needs and His heart is to bless you, but you have to live biblically for that to happen. When does the Bible say your needs will be met?

Matthew 6:25-6:34 NIV
25 "Therefore I tell you, do not worry about your life, what you will eat or drink; or about your body, what you will wear. Is not life more important than food, and the body more important than clothes? 26 Look at the birds of the air; they do not sow or reap or store away in barns, and yet your heavenly Father feeds them. Are you not much more valuable than they? 27 Who of you by worrying can add a single hour to his life?

28 "And why do you worry about clothes? See how the lilies of the field grow. They do not labor or spin. 29 Yet I tell you that not even Solomon in all his splendor was dressed like one of these. 30 If that is how God clothes the grass of the field, which is here today and tomorrow is thrown into the fire, will he not much more clothe you, O you of little faith? 31 So do not worry, saying, 'What shall we eat?' or 'What shall we drink?' or 'What shall we wear?' 32 For the pagans run after all these things, and your heavenly Father knows that you need them. 33 But seek first his kingdom and his righteousness, and all these things will be given to you as well. 34 Therefore do not worry about tomorrow, for tomorrow will worry about itself. Each day has enough trouble of its own.

What is the requirement for having our needs met? It is seeking His kingdom first. God knows very well what we need and He has no lack to take care of us, but our top priority must be to His kingdom and His destiny for our lives, not superficial things that won't last.

When does the Bible say we will be abundantly blessed?

Malachi 3:8-12 NIV
8 "Will a man rob God? Yet you rob me. "But you ask, 'How do we rob you?' "In tithes and offerings. 9 You are under a curse — the whole nation of you — because you are robbing me. 10 Bring the whole tithe into the storehouse, that there may be food in my house. Test me in this ," says the LORD Almighty,

"and see if I will not throw open the floodgates of heaven and pour out so much blessing that you will not have room enough for it. 11 I will prevent pests from devouring your crops, and the vines in your fields will not cast their fruit," says the LORD Almighty. 12 "Then all the nations will call you blessed, for yours will be a delightful land," says the LORD Almighty.

God brings more blessing than we can possibly contain when we get our priorities right. When our hearts are fully His, and everything we are and own is His, He can trust us to be truly blessed. We need to get in the place with God where we are seeking His face and not His hand. He longs for a bride who marries Him because of who He is and how wonderful He is, not for everything He could do for her.

What would you think of me if I told you I married my husband only so I could have the ring, the house, the car, and the life insurance? But truthfully, don't we sometimes have that attitude with God? When He doesn't heal us, or we can't pay the bills, or our car breaks down, or we don't live in the kind of home we'd like to, don't we sometimes feel like God is being unfair? Don't we sometimes question the value of our marriage to Him? It may seem harsh, but if those are our feelings, then we are treating God like a Sugar Daddy and to some extent, at least, we are in this marriage for what He can do for us.

On the other hand, do you think God needs a Trophy Wife? There are people who come to Christ with this attitude. They really believe God needs them and can't possibly run His kingdom without them. They think His church will never make it without their talent, opinion, gifting, or expertise. Do you think Jesus really needs someone to make Him look good and feel confident?

Colossians 1:15-20 NIV
15 He is the image of the invisible God, the firstborn over all creation. 16 For by him all things were created: things in heaven and on earth, visible and invisible, whether thrones or powers or rulers or authorities; all things were created by him and for him. 17 He is before all things , and in him all things hold together. 18 And he is the head of the body, the church; he is the beginning and the firstborn from among the dead, so that in everything he might have the supremacy. 19 For God was pleased to have all his fullness dwell in him, 20 and through him to reconcile to himself all things, whether things on earth or things in heaven, by making peace through his blood, shed on the cross.

Philippians 2:9-11 NIV
*9 Therefore God exalted him to the highest place
and gave him the name that is above every name ,*

10 that at the name of Jesus every knee should bow,
in heaven and on earth and under the earth,
11 and every tongue confess that Jesus Christ is Lord,
to the glory of God the Father.

Um . . . He sounds pretty confident to me.

What we forget is that God created us. We have nothing to offer Him that He didn't give us first. He already has it all. He is altogether lovely Himself. He knows exactly who He is and He doesn't need any ego boosting from anyone.

Please understand: He wants you to know that you're wonderful. He wants you to know He adores you. He wants you to know you have talents and gifts that He placed in you to benefit the kingdom, but you cannot manipulate Him with those things. We steal His heart by giving ours fully to Him. What follows is a marriage far more amazing than we could dream.

CHAPTER 5:
Going Deeper

1. What are some things that may have happened in our lives that distort what a healthy relationship is and how it should function?

    _____
    _____
    _____
    _____
    _____
    _____

2. Discuss with your small group (if applicable) some of the beliefs and ideas you may have been brought up with that cause similar problems. (You may also list them here so you can be aware of them and change them.)

_____

_____

_____

_____

_____

_____

3.   In a good relationship, each person does their best to meet the other's needs. The two requirements for those needs are that they be _____ and _____.

4.   What are some good questions to ask when determining whether or not to meet a need?

a. _____

b. _____

c. _____

5.   What is the motivation behind wanting a Sugar Daddy?

_____

_____

_____

_____

_____

_____

6.   What is the motivation behind wanting a Trophy Wife?

_____

_____

_____

_____

_____

_____

7.   When we view God as a Sugar Daddy, what are some things we might expect from Him?

_____

_____

_____

_____

_____

_____

8.   What are God's criteria for meeting our needs?

_____

_____

_____

_____

_____

_____

9.   What are His criteria for blessing us?

_____

_____

_____

_____

_____

_____

10.   What's a good clue that we may think of God as our Sugar Daddy?

_____

_____

_____

_____

_____

_____

11. List two passages that show why Jesus doesn't need a Trophy Wife?

a. _____

_____

_____

_____

_____

_____

b. _____

_____

_____

_____

_____

Notes / Thoughts / Prayer

_____

_____

_____

_____

_____

_____

_____

_____

_____

_____

_____

_____

_____

_____

_____

God doesn't want a one night stand;
He wants a lifelong marriage.

CHAPTER 6:
God As A Prostitute

*"I put your money on the night stand,
Uh...offering plate, now do what I want."*

A lens interprets for your mind how things are; it determines your perception of things. It may help your mind see things more clearly, or if you have on the wrong lenses, it will distort what you see until you do not perceive it clearly at all. The way your mind sees something may not be at all the way it really is. The lens through which you view your world and your relationships will determine how you see them. This is true not only of our earthly relationships but our relationship with God as well.

Seeing God as a Sugar Daddy is a huge misperception. Seeing Him as a prostitute is another one. That very statement may offend you, and truly it is horrible, but many of us are guilty of this very thing. We may each do it in a different area and in a different way, but almost everyone does it at times.

In the natural how do people treat a prostitute? What's the attitude of the person who hires a prostitute? A person goes to a prostitute to have a physical and emotional desire fulfilled. It's really an attempt to have the good things God has for us — love, affection, fulfillment, satisfaction, self-esteem — without the things that really create that — commitment, self-sacrifice, purity, faithfulness, and honor.

A prostitute receives none of the respect or honor that a spouse should. There is no faithfulness or commitment to a prostitute. There is no love. The person using a prostitute is not concerned for that prostitute's welfare or pleasure. He or she is not at all interested in the protitute's life, feelings, dreams or desires. A man having sex with a prostitute certainly does not see himself as one with her, and helping her step into her destiny is the farthest thing from his mind. The entire experience is based on his pleasure and desires; it's all about him, because he's shelling out the money. The prostitute is seen merely as an object to be rented for his usage.

Not only is the prostitute neither respected nor loved, but the sexual act with her is not the holy and wonderful experience God intended sex to be. An experience with a prostitute is not celebrated as the fulfillment of a holy covenant, nor is it an act of the most sincere intimacy that mirrors our oneness with Christ. It is an act done in secrecy and shame. It is a shameful thing to pay for something that was meant to be holy.

We can easily see the atrocity of treating any one in such a manner, especially when we realize that person was specifically created by God, in His image, with a purpose and destiny for his or her life. She is so precious that Jesus allowed Himself to be tortured and killed for her, so that she could have a new life. How much more horrible is it when we treat God Himself as a prostitute? It seems unthinkable to compare God to something that we may view with great contempt, and yet it is the very thing of which we are guilty.

Prostitution is an effort to have the pleasures of intimacy without the covenant. Do we come to God asking for the blessings of a covenant without any true commitment on our part? When a covenant was made in biblical times, it was an agreement that went far deeper than a promise. Both parties made a sincere commitment to each other concerning the matter. It was understood that each party was to do whatever it took to keep the agreement, even unto death. The breaking of a covenant resulted in severe consequences equal to whatever was lost in that covenant. That could mean repayment of the loss, the death of that person, or at times, the death of an entire tribe or even nation.

When we try to "use" God for our pleasure without having a covenant relationship with Him, we have turned Him into a prostitute. How many times have we come to God asking for the things we want, seeking our desires and pleasures, never having any concern for what is on His heart? Our prayer times can turn into a Christmas list of "I need this," and "Please work this out." Do we ever stop and ask

Him what His dreams are, what He would like us to do? I heard a gentleman say once that as he was praying one day God asked Him if He would ask, "God, what's on Your mind today?" Such a simple thought, and yet how many times do we ask that? Isn't it ironic that we have the Creator of the Universe wanting to tell us what He is thinking about, what He would like, and yet we think all that we have going on is more important? We have made our intimate times with Him so one-sided, so selfish, but there really is no one-sided intimacy.

How committed are we in this relationship? Do we come to God when we have a need or desire, just stay with Him long enough to have that met, and then leave Him there without so much as a good-bye? Worse yet, do we show up again the next time we want something, acting as though nothing is wrong, and assuming we can come and go as we please? Do we ever expect God to do whatever we want because we threw a little money on the night stand---excuse me---offering plate? Jesus repeats the words of the prophet Isaiah on this subject:

Matthew 15:8 NIV
8 These people honor me with their lips,
but their hearts are far from me.

If that is how we treat God, then saying we love Him is a lie; it's just lip service. He doesn't have our hearts.

News flash: God doesn't need our money, and He is not for sale. He's not trying to make a living; He is life itself. God doesn't want a one-night stand; He wants a lifelong marriage.

Not only can we treat God as a prostitute, but the Bible speaks clearly of ways we prostitute ourselves. The children of Israel were often guilty of this. They would say they loved the one and only true God, and then they would turn right around and worship idols brought in from other religions. They may have done it in order to make a treaty with another nation, or for financial reasons, or because they fell in love (or lust) with people in other religions. Regardless of the reason, they were, in reality, cheating on God. They were selling themselves--their loyalty and love for God — to the highest bidder.

Deuteronomy 31:16 NIV
16 And the LORD said to Moses: "You are going to rest with your fathers, and these people will soon prostitute themselves to the foreign gods of the land they are entering. They will forsake me and break the covenant I made with them.

Although sexual relations were involved in many of the pagan rituals, God was not specifically speaking of that issue. He was speaking of the fact that they were selling themselves--their loyalty and love for God—to the highest bidder.

Remember that an experience with a prostitute is an effort to have all the benefits of a covenant relationship without the responsibility of a covenant. It's a short cut, but a completely ineffective one. The Bible speaks of going to mediums and spiritists as prostitution also.

Leviticus 20:6-8 NIV
6 I will set my face against the person who turns to mediums and spiritists to prostitute himself by following them, and I will cut him off from his people. 7 Consecrate yourselves and be holy, because I am the LORD your God. 8 Keep my decrees and follow them. I am the LORD, who makes you holy.

Why is that prostitution when there's no sex involved? It's another example of trying to take a short cut, trying to take your destiny into your own hands. If we wait on God and seek His will and desire for our lives, He will guide us in the right direction.

James 1:5 NIV
5 If any of you lacks wisdom , he should ask God, who gives generously to all without finding fault, and it will be given to him.

But we don't always like to wait on the answer, do we? And sometimes we don't want a wise answer, rather we just want what we want. Let's read that whole passage and see what God says about that type of person:

James 1:2-8 NIV
2 Consider it pure joy, my brothers, whenever you face trials of many kinds, 3 because you know that the testing of your faith develops perseverance. 4 Perseverance must finish its work so that you may be mature and complete, not lacking anything. 5 If any of you lacks wisdom , he should ask God, who gives generously to all without finding fault, and it will be given to him. 6 But when he asks, he must believe and not doubt, because he who doubts is like a wave of the sea, blown and tossed by the wind. 7 That man should not think he will receive anything from the Lord; 8 he is a double-minded man, unstable in all he does.

Is it possible to prostitute, or "sell" ourselves for other things that fall short of God's best for us? Any time we put something or someone before God we have, in a way, just become a spiritual prostitute. What about not making church or our personal time with God a priority because we want other things more? Maybe work or a hobby consistently takes priority over consistently spending time with God and or being with His family?

Perhaps no one at work knows we're a Christian because we're afraid it will affect our chance for promotion. What about the relationship we've started with that really cute guy, even though we know the Bible tells us not to become involved with non-believers? It's all, in a spiritual sense, prostitution--making our choices for short term, shallow gain instead of the long term health of our relationship with God. We can't look at these sins and think they are any less horrible than physically selling our bodies on the streets. Anything that damages our relationship with Jesus is tragic. The good news is that the blood of Jesus covers all of them equally. It's no harder for Him to wash away the guilt and shame of physical prostitution than it is for Him to wash away the condemnation that comes with spiritual prostitution. He's already paid for it all.

Jesus had an incredible compassion for those caught up in prostitution. He was a champion for the value of women and the vital role they play in His kingdom. A prostitute was brought to Jesus by the hypocritical religious leaders of His day. They dragged her out in the middle of the city streets, most likely barely dressed, because she was caught in the middle of committing adultery. She was terrified and ashamed. They wanted Jesus to demand for her to be stoned, but instead He saved her life, forgave her, and told her to go and give up her life of sin. He reminded those leaders that none of them were without sin—sin that was just as bad. He called her into her destiny—it didn't matter what she had done (John 8:1-11).

It doesn't matter to God whether your prostitution has been physical or spiritual, intentional or unintentional. It all has the same consequence—spiritual death and separation from Him. God longs for us to realize He is more than a prostitute just there to please us with no commitment on our part. And His heart is broken when we prostitute ourselves to others or the material things around us. He is a jealous God who wants to be first place in our lives.

There is story after story in the Bible of women caught up in sinful lives whom Jesus loved and forgave. He gave them back the life God intended for them, and they were never the same. They became mighty women of God, full of compassion, full of the Holy Spirit, who changed their world. Jesus even chose one of these women to be the first one to see Him when He came back from the dead! Not a priest, not one of His disciples, but a woman from whom He cast seven demons! How cool is that? God can make anything new! He has a life planned for you that is so wonderful you cannot imagine it! And if you will give yourself fully to Him nothing can keep you from it.

CHAPTER 6:
Going Deeper

1. A lens determines your _____ of things.

2. Using a prostitute is an attempt to get the benefits of a covenant relationship such as:

   _____
   _____
   _____
   _____

3. What things does a covenant relationship require?

   _____
   _____
   _____

_____

_____

_____

3.   Prostitution is an effort to have the _____of intimacy without the _____.

4.   In the same way people would use a prostitute for what they want, we sometimes get _____ to God just long enough to get what we want.

5.   If we expect God to give us what we want because we pay our _____, then that is just like _____ a prostitute.

6.   Not only can we treat God as a prostitute, but we can _____ _____ ourselves when God is not our top priority.

7.   Seeking the advice of _____ or _____ _____ is another way the Bible says we prostitute ourselves.

8.   Why is it dangerous to seek the counsel of a psychic, medium, tarot card reader, or similar professions?

_____

_____

_____

_____

9.   List 2 verses that show God will tell us what we need to know.

_____

_____

_____

_____

_____

_____

10.   Describe Jesus' response to the prostitutes of His day.

_____

_____

_____

_____

_____

_____

11.   Take a few minutes to list areas in which you have "prostituted" your self and not put God first and then proactive ways in which you can change them. Take time to ask for God to forgive you and then live out the fresh start He gives you as you set your priorities daily.

_____

_____

_____

_____

_____

_____

Notes / Thoughts / Prayer

_____

_____

_____

_____

_____

_____

_____

_____

_____

When we fear someone or something,
we give it power and control over us.

CHAPTER 7:
The Double Life

"One part saint, six parts sinner."

We've all heard the incredible stories of women who have been completely dumbfounded by the discovery that the spouse they adored was actually already married, perhaps even had a home and family elsewhere. Perhaps he was a businessman who traveled frequently and had even accumulated a collection of other families. We listen to these stories amazed at the women's gullibility and appalled at the brazen audacity it must take for the husband to do such a thing. It seems when the husband is interviewed, he is surprised at the lack of understanding he receives. In his mind, the whole situation is justifiable, even reasonable: it was something that just happened, he truly does love both women and both families and couldn't give one up, no one suffered financially, he made sure to provide for both, it wasn't hurting anyone, and both families had a faithful, loving father.

Wow! Our ability to justify our selfishness and sin is astounding, isn't it? In his mind he's really done nothing wrong, and no one should be hurt; yet in the wake of his sin lies a massive trail of lies, betrayal, mistrust, confusion, broken hearts, and wounded souls.

Fortunately, these extreme cases are the exception, not the rule. Yet we have much more subtle examples of leading a double life that occur everyday, and just like that deceptive husband, we have so justified our actions that we can't even see the wrong we are doing.

CHAPTER 7: THE DOUBLE LIFE

I think one of the best ways to judge if we are doing something wrong is whether or not we would hide that act from anyone or change our behavior if someone else were there. Let's look at some examples:

Are the jokes we tell at work or when we're out with our friends the same jokes we would tell at a church picnic?

Would we respond the same way to that gorgeous co-worker if our spouses were standing in the room?

Do we find ourselves quickly finding a way to "look busy" when we hear our bosses' footsteps down the hall?

If our pastor stopped by our house unexpectedly, would we be scrambling to put away things of which we think he may not approve?

Do we spend the drive to church in an all-out battle with our kids and/or spouse but then greet everyone at church as though we are having the best day ever?

Are we mortified when the doorbell rings because we're sure the person who just rang it heard us screaming like a mad man at our spouse two seconds earlier?

When confronted with something we've said, do we find ourselves back tracking and twisting our words to make it seem not so bad?

I think one of the most hilarious examples of a subtle "double life" I ever heard of occurred during an Easter Sunday service in a close friend's very large home church. Every Sunday the pastor would bring the kids up before they were dismissed to kids' church and tell them a short story, have a little chat with them, and pray a blessing over them. The pastor was a bit ornery, and he was notorious for asking the kids (with microphone in hand), "What did your mommy and daddy tell you to be sure not to say to me today?" Well, with Easter in the Bible Belt come little girls in lots of ruffles, head to toe. He was chatting with a young girl in a dress ruffled enough to please any pageant director. With the microphone in hand and thousands listening, the conversation went much like this:

"Susie, you look so pretty today!"

"Thank you, pastor."

"That is such a beautiful dress you have on!"

"Yes, but my mom says it's a *$%@#* to iron!"

Oh, the Bible is true—your sins will be sure to find you out! Fortunately for most of us it's not at church and it's not in front of thousands of people and broadcast over the sound system!

One of the most convicting measures of character to me is, "Who you are when no one is watching, is who you really are." The truth of it is, though, that God is always with us, isn't He? We truly are never alone.

As we examine our hearts, are we living a double life? Do we profess our undying love and faithfulness to God at church and in front of our Christian friends but then turn around and "cheat" on Him at work or with our friends who we would insist have lower standards than ours? Do we justify it by believing that overall we're good people and we're not really hurting anyone? Perhaps we believe that living a Christian lifestyle in a secular world is just unrealistic.

Some people believe that compromising their values is actually necessary as a witnessing tool. They believe it makes them more approachable to others and builds a bridge between them and those who don't know Jesus personally. We can't compartmentalize our relationship with God. We can't reserve Him for little sections of our lives where we feel He's appropriate. That's like acting like we're married only when it suits us. What kind of jerks do that? And do we truly love our spouse if that's how we're acting? I want the kind of husband who would show my picture off and brag about how awesome I am even if he were at the Miss America pageant! I'm supposed to be the center of his life! If he's ashamed of me anywhere, then he's not the kind of man I want and our relationship is not what it should be. It is a pitiful spouse who would put up with that, and yet how many times do we treat God that way? He won't put up with it, either.

My husband had a teacher in high school who would take off her wedding ring whenever she chaperoned for out-of-town trips. She would act like it was no big deal and say she really loved her husband, but that was a lie. In the end, she ended up being fired from her position for sleeping with one of her students, and her husband committed suicide. I guess that whole line about it not hurting anyone just isn't true, huh? We may not take our wedding rings off, but how about our cross (or anything that we would normally wear that associates us with Christ)? Do we reconsider wearing it when it may offend someone or when we think it might affect our sales? Do we carefully avoid any mention of being in a committed relationship with Jesus because it might affect what others think of us? I don't think we need to obnoxiously brag about being married--in the natural or spiritually---but we need to consistently be the same person, regardless of our environment.

Sadly, many of our churches nowadays are going down that same road. They are trying to become "culturally relevant" by keeping everything in the church "low pressure" and easily acceptable. The gospel has become an "I'm okay, you're okay" gospel, not one of repentance, dedication, and destiny in the kingdom. They shun the supernatural because it may offend or confuse. Meanwhile the world delves deeper and deeper into the satanic side of the supernatural searching for something to answer their questions. Unfortunately, people can be culturally relevant all the way to hell. There is nothing, nor anyone more relevant to the needs in anyone's life than Jesus Christ. We need to love people enough to tell them the truth with great love. He is all they truly need.

I am not promoting an ultra-religious, holier-than-thou attitude at all. I think we Christians need to live our lives as approachable, humble, loving people. We would do well to drop all the "Christian-ease" language and just let our relationship with the Lord and our love for him overflow from us naturally. Religion is what is awkward to people, but Jesus is who they deeply desire. It's important that we don't confuse the two.

The Bible speaks very clearly of the consequences of living a double life.

Mark 8:38 NIV
38 If anyone is ashamed of me and my words in this adulterous and sinful generation, the Son of Man will be ashamed of him.

Truly, when we lead a double life it is not in an effort to relate to those around us. We change who we are and we hide the truth because we are ashamed of God and our relationship with Him. We are afraid of ridicule and rejection. And in the end it is because we care more about what mere men think of us than what a perfect, holy, loving God thinks.

It's called fear of man, and it is probably the most crippling fear we can ever have. Nothing can do more damage to our destinies than fear of man. Even if no one ever really rejects or ridicules us because of our relationship with God, the fear that they will can keep us from all the amazing things God has in store for us. When we fear someone or something, we give it power and control over us.

The Bible puts it this way:

Proverbs 29:25 NIV
25 Fear of man will prove to be a snare,
but whoever trusts in the LORD is kept safe.

Here are some other powerful thoughts on fear:

Franklin D. Roosevelt said, *"We have nothing to fear but fear itself."*

Veer Sharma:

F False
E Evidence
A Appearing
R Real

Ambrose Redmoon: Courage is not the absence of fear, but the judgement that something else is more important than fear.

Fear of man has power over us only when we deem man's opinion worth more than God's. The irony of that is that we can never please everyone all the time. Part of the reason people criticize others is to bring them down to their level, to make sure no one ever rises above them so that they themselves can have an excuse for the way they live. It may be their sin they are excusing, or their laziness, or even just their mediocrity. God calls us to live above that. The Bible says that the Gospel is the fragrance of life to those who believe and the stench of death to those who don't (2 Corinthians 2:16). When we understand the value of what we are offering them (even if it is only by the example of the life we live), the fear simply fades in comparison.

Romans 1:16 NIV
16 I am not ashamed of the gospel, because it is the power of God for the salvation
of everyone who believes: first for the Jew, then for the Gentile.

When we understand what the gospel is—the very power of God to save that person from an eternity in hell and the very power of God to bring that person into the incredible destiny God has for him or her, then the chance that you may be rejected or ridiculed is not even worth your consideration.

The only fear the Bible endorses is the fear of the Lord. It's not an unreasonable fear of a hateful God that is out to get you, but a holy reverence for an all-powerful God who is perfectly loving, merciful, just, and fierce all at the same time. That fear is an absolute necessity, and God says that is the very beginning of wisdom (Psalm 111:10,

Proverbs 9:10) and that He delights in them that fear Him (Psalm 147:11). There is verse after verse telling of the blessings we receive when we fear the Lord.

The good news is we don't have to live with a fear of man. When we understand who we are and the power that is within us, that fear seems just silly! Let's look at God's perceptions of our fears:

1 Peter 3:14-16 NIV
14 But even if you should suffer for what is right, you are blessed. "Do not fear what they fear ; do not be frightened." 15 But in your hearts set apart Christ as Lord. Always be prepared to give an answer to everyone who asks you to give the reason for the hope that you have. But do this with gentleness and respect, 16 keeping a clear conscience, so that those who speak maliciously against your good behavior in Christ may be ashamed of their slander.

1 John 4:18 NIV
18 There is no fear in love. But perfect love drives out fear , because fear has to do with punishment. The one who fears is not made perfect in love.

When you understand who you are, that perfect love of your father drives out that fear. We are to have the very character of God in us — His DNA because we are His children. Fear is not part of His DNA!

2 Timothy 1:7-8 NKJV
7 For God has not given us a spirit of fear, but of power and of love and of a sound mind.
8 Therefore do not be ashamed of the testimony of our Lord.

Romans 8:15 NIV
15 For you did not receive a spirit that makes you a slave again to fear , but you received the Spirit of sonship. And by him we cry, "Abba, Father."

Whoo-hoo! God hasn't given us a spirit of fear, or as the NIV puts it, "a spirit of timidity"! It doesn't matter what your personality type is, God has called you to be bold, to be a fearless warrior! When God commissioned Joshua to take the land that was inhabited by giants (a land that not even Moses would press in to take), He gave him this command:

Deuteronomy 31:6 NIV
6 Be strong and courageous . Do not be afraid or terrified because of them, for the LORD your God goes with you; he will never leave you nor forsake you.

We have that same promise today! We don't need to fear anyone but God — and He's on our side! Every time we face a situation in which we fear ridicule or rejection, every time we think we may lose our job or our friends if we live our Christian life out loud, He's right there with us. Be strong! Be courageous! We have nothing of value to lose and the kingdom of God to gain. Everywhere our feet land we should be claiming land for God. If God is for us, who can be against us (Romans 8:31)?

Don't lead a double life. Don't let fear steal your destiny. Fear has power over us only when we give that power to it. Fear of anyone or anything besides God is a lie, and a lie has power only when we come into agreement with it (Shannon Schreyer). Break off the lies. Rise above them. We hold the power of life and death in our tongues (Proverbs 18:21). Speak life! We have life itself to offer those around us. Don't be ashamed. Be strong and courageous, for the Lord our God is with us!

CHAPTER 7:
Going Deeper

1. A good way to judge if you are leading a "double life" is:

   _____

   _____

   _____

   _____

   _____

   _____

2. Who you are when _____ is watching is who you really are.

3. Using God in only the areas that you think are appropriate is _____ _____ Him.

4. Mark 8:38 says that if we are _____ of Christ and His

_____ in our lives, then He will be ashamed of us.

5. Often we don't lead a double life in an effort to relate to those around us; we change who we are and how we act because we are _____ _____ of our relationship with God.

6. When we care more about what those around us think than what God thinks, it is called _____ of _____.

7. Proverbs 29:25 "_____ of man will prove to be a _____, but whoever _____ in the Lord is kept safe."

8. Many times people bring others _____ to their level, so that they themselves can have an _____ for the way they live.

9. 2 Corinthians 2:16 says the gospel is the fragrance of _____ to those who believe and the stench of _____ to those who won't.

10. Why should we not be ashamed of Jesus and His gospel?

    _____

    _____

    _____

    _____

    _____

    _____

11. The only fear the Bible endorses is the fear of _____.

12. The fear of the Lord is the very beginning of _____. (Psalm 111:10, Proverbs 9:10)

13.   God _____in them that fear Him. (Psalm 147:11)

14.   Deuteronomy 31:5-6 "Be _____ and _____.
        Do not be afraid or terrified because of them, for the Lord your God
        goes with you; He will _____ leave you or _____
        you."

Woohoo!

THOUGHTS TO LIVE BY:

"We have nothing to fear but fear itself."
Franklin D. Roosevelt

F   False
E   Evidence
A   Appearing
R   Real

"Courage is not the absence of fear, but the judgement that
something else is more important than fear."
Ambrose Redmoon

VERSES TO FIGHT FEAR:
1 Peter 3:14-17, 1 John 4:18, 2 Timothy 1:7-8, Romans 8:15, Romans 8:31

Notes / Thoughts/ Prayer

_____
_____
_____
_____
_____

We have to be very careful that what we truly treasure is Jesus Himself, not how He makes us feel or what He does for us.

CHAPTER 8:

The Out-of-Town Affair

"I love going away for a wild weekend, but it's just not for every day."

You plan the trip, save your money, and spend hours online checking flights and car rentals. You've looked at a million hotel rooms for just the right one. You count down the days and daydream with anticipation about the big weekend. You've taken time off work and everything else can wait! You wonder what will happen. Will he touch you? It makes you tingle just to think about how he overwhelms you at times. Will you see things you haven't seen before? Will he whisper sweet things in your ear? You determine to tell him all the ways you love him. You're so excited just to have some uninterrupted time to be intimate with him and focus on your relationship. It seems like forever since you've been away with him. You're determined to let loose and lose all your inhibitions. You're gonna dance all night and get as drunk as can be. Who cares what people think?They don't know you, anyway! This weekend you're going to give yourself completely to him.

Oh, I'm sorry. Did you think I was talking about going away for some wild sexual affair? No, silly! I was talking about going to a CHURCH CONFERENCE!

Seriously, now, don't we think like that sometimes? (Yes, you can go back and read it again, now that you know what I'm talking about!) Okay, now that you know I'm not writing a sleazy romance novel, let's go for some more clarification.

You must understand that above anything, I treasure my relationship with my Lord, and I have a passion for being in His presence. Through the years that my husband and I have pastored, we have urged our church body to make it a priority to be anywhere God is pouring out His presence and power. This may be conferences, retreats, advances, schools of ministry, or services at a church full of His presence. We let them know when these events are taking place, we reserve blocks of hotel rooms, we announce, we promote, we scholarship, we carpool, we save, and we sacrifice to be in God's presence and have His Spirit imparted to us.

Some people would argue that one doesn't need to go away anywhere to be in God's presence. Theoretically, that's true. We have been incredibly blessed with the presence of God in our own church, and yet we gladly make pilgrimages to anywhere we know that God is pouring out His presence. There is something that steals God's heart when we lay down our pride, give up our control of how we think God should do things, and make being transformed in the presence of God our top priority. It's the story of Jacob who wrestled with God all night, refusing to let Him go until God touched him (Genesis 32:22-32). It's the woman who had the issue of blood for twelve years, but risked ridicule and rejection to press through the crowd just to touch Jesus' garment, because she knew if she could just touch Him, she would be changed (Luke 8: 43-48).

In spite of the high value we put on being in the manifest (tangible) presence of God, we have noticed a very disturbing trend among some of those who attend such meetings. We call them "conference junkies." In other words, they have become addicted to conferences, retreats, etc. These people seem to never miss a special event. Somehow they always manage to get off work, have the money, and buy the T-shirt. At first glance you would think this a wonderfully noble trait—that they are addicted to the presence of God, and yet as you study the situation, you sadly realize that is not the case. It is not God's presence they are addicted to, but the "high" they get from the conference. Although we should all come back refreshed and on fire from these events, the true test of whether or not we were transformed is the lasting change that has taken place. The proof is in the fruit, so to speak.

So often we see people who seem to have been radically touched by God at an event, and yet when they come home, they seem to "crash" and go through "withdrawal" until they get another "fix." There is no change in their lifestyles. They rarely attend church gatherings, their financial giving doesn't show God or His church as a priority, they are short tempered, anxious, impetuous, and their life is in emotional turmoil almost immediately upon their return.

They seem to have written down every word the conference speaker spoke and "amened" until they were hoarse, but upon their return home they don't feel like their own pastor, close friends, or family members have anything to say worth hearing, and if they bring any correction or concerns to them at all, they are offended. During the conference they made huge promises to God and many times to others, but sadly those promises only last as long as the conference itself. Sounds a lot like that weekend fling, doesn't it? In the heat of the moment a lot of false promises are made, but when everything calms down the promise maker doesn't have the commitment or maturity to keep their word. That once passionate love comes back into town and acts like they never saw the other person. It's really heartbreaking for the other person who thought they meant every word, and when that happens enough times, they quickly trust no one.

It's just as heartbreaking for Jesus. Of course, He has the advantage of knowing whether or not you mean it, but being lied to still hurts. How must He feel when we act so passionately in love with Him, so full of His Spirit when we are away from our home environment, but as soon as we get home we act completely bored with Him, or never come to be with Him? When that is how we act, we either didn't mean a thing we said, or we are now operating out of the fear of man, simply complacency, or a lack of discipline. To be blunt, we are being hypocritical, immature, and weak. Ooh, those are strong words.

We have to be very careful that what we truly treasure is Jesus Himself, not how He makes us feel or what He does for us. I once had one of the most disappointing and heart-breaking experiences of my life because I was confusing these. Our church had just ended a forty day fast and my husband and I flew to Pennsylvania to attend a wonderful conference. Having just finished the fast, I was very focused on having a life changing experience during our time there. In the natural, I am a high energy, fast-spoken, and demonstrative person, while my husband is a quieter, easy-going, and very relational guy. But when the Spirit hits us we seem to switch personalities. My husband can be drunk as a skunk in the Holy Spirit, laugh like crazy, or spin across the room. I, on the other hand, seem to be just the opposite. Although I may have physical manifestations at times, I have never done any of those things, and usually, I am basically quiet and would rather be off in a corner praying by myself.

The way God touched us during this conference followed suit. It was an awesome time, but I really was hoping and praying for God to radically touch me, and in my heart I wanted it to be in a very tangible way. I was looking for this emotionally and physically overwhelming experience. I got nothing. I spent the last prayer time lying under the grand piano frustrated with God and spending more time feeling sorry for myself than loving on Him. I really was angry with God because I thought it was unfair, especially after a forty day fast (which I stuck to, but my husband had to quit on day three because he got horribly sick—go figure)! To be totally honest, I got up from prayer that night furious with God and I had the audacity to tell Him, "I don't know how you can say you love me and that I'm your bride. I HAVE a husband who loves me, and if I ask HIM to touch me, HE DOES!" YIKES! Obviously God is incredibly patient and merciful because I'm still around to write this book! I gave God the silent treatment for about three days and then God quietly asked me, "Would you like to know why I didn't touch you the way you wanted?" Knowing that my behavior was wrong, even though I desperately wished it were justified, I meekly said yes. He responded, "You wanted to dictate how and when I touch you and even thought not eating for forty days obligated me to do what you wanted. But I'm not a prostitute and I won't be told what to do and how to do it, nor can I be manipulated or "paid" off by anyone's actions." Boom. I had valued having a physical experience above Jesus Himself. Sounds like caring more about the wild weekend than you really do about the person, huh? I will tell you that what He taught me by NOT doing what I asked was far more valuable than what I would have received if I had gotten what I asked for.

I have many people come to me for prayer or counsel because they don't "feel" God. If they don't feel Him, they think there is something wrong, or there is a distance between them and God. At times that may be true, but we have to be very careful not to measure our relationships by our feelings. I dare say if every married couple only stayed married when they felt like it, we'd all be divorced! Love isn't just about feelings. It is about commitment and relationship. The same is true with our relationship with Jesus. It's not going to be one constant "high." God wants a maturity and depth to our relationship that goes beyond getting our way and lets God deal with us the way He knows is best.

There was a time a year or so before my "pouting piano experience" that God gave me the most precious, personal encounter with Him. At the time I was in a season of pursuing intimacy with God but was also a full-time teacher with four children ages one to six. My husband was pastoring full time about 30 minutes from our home. It was a crazy time! Because of my husband's job and the distance it was from home, the great majority of caring for the kids was my responsibility. (Our children attended school and childcare in the same private school in which I taught.) To be completely honest, I felt very left out when it came to having these huge God encounters that everyone else, including my husband, were having because it always seemed I had a lapful of kids! I had come to the point where I decided that since God didn't touch me the way He did my husband, He must adore my husband and merely tolerate me only because my husband loved me. I know that's horrible, but I'm being completely honest.

During that time a small group from our church traveled about 11 hours in our van to a conference in Denver, CO. Before the evening session we were in the sanctuary just chatting and singing along with the band as they did their sound check. Suddenly the most amazing fragrance filled the area where we were standing. We thought perhaps someone had opened some anointing oil or such, but after checking around we could find no one who had. We realized that it was the physical fragrance of God. It was the first time any of us had experienced that and it was absolutely captivating. You could literally walk in and out of the fragrance also, as though it was contained in a certain area.

We spent our drive home from that conference just talking about all that had happened and all that God had done in our lives. We would ride for hours at a time praying and worshipping. During one of those periods that same fragrance came into the van. It was incredible!

A night or two after we arrived home I was soaking in the tub (the only place a mother with young children is alone!) and reading a great book called, "Elijah, Anointed and Stressed" by Jeff Lucas (seemed to be the appropriate book for my life at the time). I was thinking about the conference and that supernatural fragrance of God that we had experienced. Because my husband and others were at both the church and in the van, I was wondering to myself if, once again, I had only been allowed to experience such an amazing manifestation because I caught it on the "shirt tail" of others, especially my husband. At that very moment, as I was absolutely the only human in the room, the fragrance of God came in that bathroom! I'm so disappointed at my reaction now, but I just felt so comfortable that He was there, that I stopped reading and said out loud, "Oh! Hi!" and then went back to reading. Pitiful, I know! But at that moment I knew without any doubt that God had come into that room JUST FOR ME! He didn't come because anyone else was there, He didn't come because I was doing anything super-spiritual, or because I was in an amazing service where He was just messing everyone up. He came just to be with me. I KNEW He loved ME for ME. It was a huge turning point in my relationship with Him. It wasn't loud, uncontrollable, or even extremely unusual, but it was so perfectly personal it changed me forever.

God longs for someone who is passionate for Him. But that may mean dancing and shouting or that may mean quietly weeping in a corner. He longs for us to crave *Him*, not just how He can make us feel. Times of refreshing are absolutely necessary, but intimacy with Christ cannot be limited to weekends away. Letting down our inhibitions to worship Him like children shouldn't happen just when no one we know is watching. We need to give ourselves over to Him fully all the time, not just at special events.

I think these lyrics by Chris Tomlin should be how we live:

> *I want to live like there's no tomorrow,*
> *I want to dance like no one's around,*
> *I want to sing like nobody's listening*
> *Before I lay my body down.*
>
> *I want to give like I have plenty*
> *I want to love like I'm not afraid*
> *I want to be the man I was meant to be*
> *I want to be the way I was made.*

Our relationship with Jesus can't be just a wild weekend affair that we zoom out of town to once in awhile. We were created for so much more. Be what you were made to be: a full-time, passionate, committed bride who loves her groom consistently and in every way. Then He will truly say, "You have stolen my heart, my bride!" (Song of Songs 4:9).

CHAPTER 8:
Going Deeper

1.   Two examples of pursuing the touch of God are:

     a. _____

         _____

         _____

         _____

         _____

         _____

     b. _____

         _____

         _____

         _____

         _____

         _____

2. Three things that are required in order to be transformed by God are:

    a. _____

    _____

    _____

    b. _____

    _____

    _____

    c. _____

    _____

    _____

3. What is a nickname for people who are addicted to the "high" on the emotion of a conference?

    _____

4. How can you tell that the "high" they experienced was merely a "fix" and not transformative?

    _____

    _____

    _____

    _____

    _____

    _____

5. We know transformation is real because the _____ is in the _____.

6. Usually, we act one way at a church or a conference and differently at home because of _____ of _____.

7. We have to be very careful that what we truly treasure is _____,
   not just how He _____.

8. Love is not just about _____. It's about _____
   and _____.

9. God wants _____ and _____in our relationship.

When we give ourselves fully and passionately to Him all the time, that's when
He says, "You have stolen my heart, my bride!" (Song of Songs 4:9)

I want to live like there's no tomorrow,
I want to dance like no one's around,
I want to sing like nobody's listening
Before I lay my body down.

I want to give like I have plenty
I want to love like I'm not afraid
I want to be the man I was meant to be
I want to be the way I was made.

Chris Tomlin—"The Way I Was Made"—Arriving

Notes / Thoughts / Prayer

_____
_____
_____
_____
_____
_____
_____
_____

Excellence exposes mediocrity, truth exposes lies, love exposes hate, generosity exposes greed, and passion exposes complacency.

CHAPTER 9:
The Fairy Tale

*"Someday my prince will come, and
I will have the perfect life!"*

Fairy tales are wonderful things. Everyone needs a little break from reality now and then. When we're young we call them fairy tales; when we're grown we call them "chick flicks." We gasp at the injustice of the characters' situations, laugh at the way in which fate brings them together, protest when the antagonist tries to tear them apart, and cheer when love triumphs and they finally kiss! Then there's the collective sigh as the lights come up and everyone says, "Oh, that was a good movie!"

We love a happy ending. If Prince Charming doesn't rescue Cinderella and give her the perfect, carefree life, we hate the story. It doesn't matter how unrealistic the story line may be; we are satisfied only if it turns out the way we want it.

There's only one problem with a fairy tale: it is always fiction, and attempting to live in a fairy tale is the most frustrating life imaginable. Not only is this true in an earthly relationship, but also in our relationship with Jesus. It is true that when Christ returns for us and we go to spend eternity with Him, it will be the perfect, painless life. But many of us are looking for that to happen in this life, while we are living in a world under Satan's curse. God is calling us to be overcomers, more than conquerors, but in order to be overcomers, there must be something to overcome; in order to be more than conquerors, there has to be something for us to conquer. If we live our lives trying to avoid this reality we will live our lives always disappointed, always frustrated, always confused. We will spend our lives furious at the injustices to which we see ourselves as the victim.

God's plan is to give us an abundant life (John 10:10)and to give us peace that goes beyond the world's understanding (Philippians 4:7). He has "...plans to prosper us and not to harm us, to give us a hope and a future" (Jeremiah 29:11). But in order to have all that, we have to quit living in a fantasy world. We have to give up childish ideas and be ready to have a mature relationship that is steadfast through all of life's storms, whether earthly or spiritual. The lies we are taught in fairy tales must be exposed. The only way to destroy a lie is with the truth, so we are going to look at the lies a fairy tale perpetuates and break their power over us with the truth.

Lie #1: "I am the poor, mistreated victim. I have no hope but to wait for my Prince Charming to come and rescue me."

Wow! I've spent so many hours with people who cling to this lie! They spend more time and energy on being the victim than it would take to be the victor! It's really a control issue to insist on being the victim. If I am the victim, then I surely can't be expected to change my life! People certainly can't expect me to do anything for myself or be responsible for my own thoughts or actions! So I get to spend my whole life expecting people to feel sorry for me, take care of me, and never hold me accountable to be the powerful person I was created to be. Well, guess what, no one has an excuse to stay a victim. Although God is grieved by any kind of abuse that anyone goes through, and He is saddened if others have mistreated you and tried to stomp out the life He has planned for you, He is not overwhelmed or discouraged. He has only good plans for you and is well able to accomplish them in you. Give up the excuses. You're about to be amazing! Here are some of the scriptures that refute the victim lies and show the truth of what God says about you:

> **Romans 3:23-24 NIV**
> *23 for all have sinned and fall short of the glory of God, 24 and are justified freely by his grace through the redemption that came by Christ Jesus.*

> **John 8:32 NIV**
> *32 Then you will know the truth, and the truth will set you free .*

> **Philippians 4:13 NIV**
> *13 I can do all things through Christ who strengthens me.*

> **Philippians 1:6 NIV**
> *6 He who began a good work in me will be faithful to complete it.*

A few other stories that give us powerful examples of people escaping the victim mindset are: 2 Kings 7:3 (4 lepers), Luke 8:43 (the woman with the issue of blood) 1 Samuel 17 (David and Goliath) Luke 8 (Mary Magdelene).

We all have sinned and made our own bad choices, but we can choose to be forgiven, be free, and come up higher.

Lie #2: "When my Prince Charming comes, He will see how perfect I am, and He will never want me to change. True love means never having to change."

I love the old saying, "God loves us just the way we are and too much to let us stay that way." The grace of God doesn't require us to become perfect before we give our lives to Him, but the purpose and calling God has for each of us will take us from a forgiven lump of coal to a stunning diamond ready to be put on display. God describes Himself as a potter (Isaiah 64:8). He takes clay and molds it into a vessel for His use and pleasure. It's not a matter of punishment, but of refinement. It's the journey of coming fully into the destinies that God planned for us even before we were born, of becoming mature sons and daughters of God. Becoming like Him in thinking and character allows us into a greater intimacy with Him, because it removes any differences that would keep a distance between us. Being transformed into Christ's image may be a challenging journey for us, but it will bring incredible joy and confidence into our lives.

Romans 12:2 NIV
2 Do not conform any longer to the pattern of this world, but be transformed by the renewing of your mind.

2 Corinthians 3:18 NIV
18 And we, who with unveiled faces all reflect the Lord's glory, are being transformed into his likeness with ever-increasing glory, which comes from the Lord, who is the Spirit.

Leviticus 11:44 NIV
44 I am the LORD your God; consecrate yourselves and be holy, because I am holy.

Lie #3: "Because He will want to pamper and take care of me as His princess, He will never expect anything of me."

Deep in the heart of every woman is a desire to be protected and cherished. There is absolutely nothing wrong with that, and that desire was created in us by God Himself. But when Father God desired a bride for His son, and when Jesus longed for a bride for Himself, they didn't have a weak, lazy bride in mind. A good marriage is not one-sided. It is a partnership where both spouses are strong and powerful. They complete each other, challenge each other, and encourage each other. God's desire isn't to do everything for us. He has put talents and abilities in each of us that He wants us to use to become "co-creators" with Him. He loves to see us try something new, do something challenging, and succeed! Just being a "kept wife" is such an unfulfilling life! Jesus and you are meant to be a team together. Bill Johnson, senior leader of Bethel Church in Redding, CA, says, "Jesus is looking for a bride whose body is in proportion to her head." That's a great statement! It's not that we become deity, but He made us to be mighty through Him, and He wants a partner!

Luke 12:48 NIV
48 From everyone who has been given much, much will be demanded; and from the one who has been entrusted with much, much more will be asked.

Deuteronomy 8:18 NIV
18 But remember the LORD your God, for it is he who gives you the <u>ability to produce wealth</u>, and so confirms his covenant, which he swore to your ancestors, as it is today.

Exodus 36:2 NIV
2 Then Moses summoned Bezalel and Oholiab and every skilled person to whom the LORD had given ability and who was willing to come and do the work.

Ephesians 2:10 NIV
10 For we are God's handiwork, created in Christ Jesus to do good works, which God prepared in advance for us to do.

Matthew 25 tells the story of the three servants who were each given an amount of money according to their ability to steward it. (Notice they each had ability.) The only one who was not rewarded and also had his money taken away was the one who just buried what the master had given him and did nothing with it. The Bible says that God gives "seed to the sower" (2 Corinthians 9:10). God is absolutely our provider, but notice that He is giving seed to the *sower*. There is a partnership and work to be done. He has also created us to feel fulfilled when we partner with Him to establish His kingdom.

Lie #4: "Once we are together, I will have everything I ever wanted."

Once you become the bride of Christ you will absolutely have everything you need, but not necessarily everything you want. This generation, especially here in the

United States, has a very distorted view of the difference between needs and wants. The Christian life is a bit of a paradox in this area. On one hand, we have the most extravagantly generous father, but He is at the same time not one to be manipulated by our childish greed. God lacks absolutely nothing, so lavishing us with every good thing is no challenge for Him.

His word says in Psalm 84:11, "For the LORD God is a sun and shield; the LORD bestows favor and honor; no good thing does he withhold from those whose walk is blameless." Luke 12:32 says that He is pleased to give us the kingdom. He reminds us that if our earthly fathers, who are evil, give us good gifts, then how much more generous will He be (Matthew 7:11)? His concern is not so much toward what we have or don't have, as much as it is how we feel about those things. The question is, "Did you marry Him for Him or for just what He could give you?" He wants always to be the center of your heart, your greatest treasure.

Philippians 4:11-13 NIV
11 I am not saying this because I am in need, for I have learned to be content whatever the circumstances. 12 I know what it is to be in need, and I know what it is to have plenty. I have learned the secret of being content in any and every situation, whether well fed or hungry, whether living in plenty or in want. 13 I can do everything through him who gives me strength.

Matthew 6:19-21 NIV
19 Do not store up for yourselves treasures on earth, where moth and rust destroy, and where thieves break in and steal. 20 But store up for yourselves treasures in heaven, where moth and rust do not destroy, and where thieves do not break in and steal. 21 For where your treasure is, there your heart will be also.

James 1:9 NIV
9 The brother in humble circumstances ought to take pride in his high position.

So often God is giving us what we need and what we truly desire but it comes in a package that we don't recognize. It's not until later, when we can look back and see the whole picture, that we understand He was "working all things together for good" and blessing us far more than we could understand.

Lie #5: "Once we are together, I will never have another problem."

Oh, how I wish this lie were true! Wouldn't that be awesome? Then everyone in the world would be Christians. Unfortunately, we aren't immediately transported to heaven the moment we give our lives to Christ. We still remain in this world, in the same body, in the same family, at the same job, with the same bills and budget. We are completely forgiven instantly, and many times there are amazing miracles that God works out in the circumstances of our lives, but most of our lives are transformed over time and by our choices. I'm deeply moved by the passage toward the end of Hebrews 11 where the writer lists the horrors endured by many of God's children. Hebrews 11 is called the "faith chapter," or the "hall of faith" because it gives so many examples of these men and women of incredible faith who endured things that were cruel and unfair. And yet in verse 38 God's assessment of them was that "the world was not worthy of them." That is really powerful and encouraging to me. They weren't persecuted because God was angry with them or they were out of relationship with Him. There's a much bigger picture at work here. We live in an unredeemed world, full of horrible acts, because God values free will even above right and wrong. He always gives people a choice. He is not controlling or manipulative. He wants lovers, not slaves. And with that freedom many make terrible choices that devastate others. The truth to hold onto is that God is able to heal all things, and He is not uncaring nor inactive. He is always working things for our good even when we can't see it (Romans 8:28).

1 Peter 4:12-13 NIV
12 Dear friends, do not be surprised at the painful trial you are suffering, as though something strange were happening to you. 13 But rejoice that you participate in the sufferings of Christ, so that you may be overjoyed when his glory is revealed.

James 1:2-8 NIV
2 Consider it pure joy, my brothers, whenever you face trials of many kinds, 3 because you know that the testing of your faith develops perseverance. 4 Perseverance must finish its work so that you may be mature and complete, not lacking anything. 5 If any of you lacks wisdom, he should ask God, who gives generously to all without finding fault, and it will be given to him. 6 But when he asks, he must believe and not doubt, because he who doubts is like a wave of the sea, blown and tossed by the wind. 7 That man should not think he will receive anything from the Lord; 8 he is a double-minded man, unstable in all he does.

Jeremiah 29:11 NIV
11 "For I know the plans I have for you," says the Lord. "Plans to prosper you and not to harm you. Plans to give you a hope and a future."

Lie #6: "Once I am a princess, everyone will love me!"

Life would be so much easier if this lie were true, too. Alas, it is still just a lie. People don't always make the right choice, nor behave the right way, nor like all the things that are good for them. It is the most ironic thing that when we are actually doing our best to do what is right and to love everyone around us, we will have people who hate us for those very reasons. It is a rare person, (sadly, even a rare Christian) who is open to seeing his or her own faults. But is an undeniable principle that excellence exposes mediocrity, truth exposes lies, love exposes hate, generosity exposes greed, and passion exposes complacency. People don't like to be exposed. It's not that we are even trying to expose anything. It's just what happens when Jesus "leaks" out of us. Many will be offended, but some, those precious ones open to Jesus, will be drawn to us because they have found in us this Jesus for whom they have searched and longed all their lives.

In my experience I have found the most effective way for me to deal with those offended is to understand that I am really not the problem. Obviously, I need to take responsibility for any wrong actions or attitudes on my part, but when I have truly behaved in a godly manner and people are still furious with me, I come to understand that to them I am, as my husband puts it, "doom perfume." The fragrance of Christ is repulsive to them because they are rejecting Him. When this happens, I decide to just "Teflon" their hatred off. Just like an egg slides off a non-stick pan, I let the comments, looks, and other actions slide off of me so that I can continue to love them without any of their "junk" sticking to me. If they hated Jesus, who was perfect, I'm certainly not going to make them love me.

1 John 3:13 NIV
13 Do not be surprised , my brothers, if the world hates you.

John 15:18-19 NIV
18 If the world hates you, keep in mind that it hated me first . 19 If you belonged to the world, it would love you as its own. As it is, you do not belong to the world, but I have chosen you out of the world. That is why the world hates you.

2 Corinthians 2:14-16 NIV
14 But thanks be to God, who always leads us in triumphal procession in Christ and through us spreads everywhere the fragrance of the knowledge of him. 15 For we are to God the aroma of Christ among those who are being saved and those who are perishing. 16 To the one we are the smell of death; to the other, the fragrance of life . And who is equal to such a task?

Lie #7: "Once I begin my new life, my old life will miraculously change and be perfect, too."

This was already addressed somewhat when we discussed needing to change. Some of us would love for our lives to completely change. We have huge messes we have created, or that others have created for us, and we desperately want rescued. And again, it is true, that when we come into alignment with God's heart for us He will move heaven and hell to bring about His purposes in our lives. But a large part of our destiny is learning and growing into who He created us to be. Our character and Christ-likeness is formed as we deal with the situations in which we live. We live a powerful life when we love others supernaturally through painful situations, when we choose to do the right thing when the wrong thing seems immensely easier. His greatest desire is to see us perfected in maturity and intimacy with Him, and that is accomplished through a lifelong journey, not through an instant impartation.

Sometimes even the favor of God can bring on persecution. It was certainly true in the lives of Jesus, His apostles, and even His mother! Look at the life of Mary: She was a young girl, probably around the age of 16. She was a godly young woman, a virgin, and a faithful Jew. She was doing all the right things and obviously loved God and desired to please Him. When God chose to have Mary be the biological mother of Jesus, it was an honor. To birth the Messiah was the most favored position any Jewish woman could have, but no one thought the mother of the Messiah was going to be an unwed, teenage mom. The favor of God put Mary in a place of ridicule and persecution. I'm sure hardly anyone believed her story. Even the man she was engaged to almost left her because of it. God sent an angel to convince him, but He didn't do that for everyone else in Mary's life. Mary had to learn to live her life secure in God's love for her regardless of how everyone else treated her. What God thought of her had to far outweigh what anyone else thought of her. She had to be completely convinced of the destiny God had given her and live her life fulfilling that, regardless of the ridicule. Just think of the loss if Mary had aborted Jesus to avoid others' ridicule and criticism, or killed herself because she just couldn't take the unfair treatment. Our destinies are far too important to let the world talk us out of them. We can't live by our feelings or worry about what others say or do. We are called by God to be great men and women of God, and that has to be our focus. Take the advice of the writer of Hebrews:

Hebrews 12:1-3 NIV

1 Therefore, since we are surrounded by such a great cloud of witnesses, let us throw off everything that hinders and the sin that so easily entangles. And let us run with perseverance the race marked out for us, 2 fixing our eyes on Jesus, the pioneer and perfecter of faith. For the joy set before him he endured the cross, scorning its shame, and sat down at the right hand of the throne of God.

3 Consider him who endured such opposition from sinners, so that you will not grow weary and lose heart.

2 Corinthians 12:7-10 NIV

7 To keep me from becoming conceited because of these surpassingly great revelations, there was given me a thorn in my flesh, a messenger of Satan, to torment me. 8 Three times I pleaded with the Lord to take it away from me. 9 But he said to me, "My grace is sufficient for you, for my power is made perfect in weakness." Therefore I will boast all the more gladly about my weaknesses, so that Christ's power may rest on me. 10 That is why, for Christ's sake, I delight in weaknesses, in insults, in hardships, in persecutions, in difficulties. For when I am weak, then I am strong.

Romans 8:18 NIV

18 I consider that our present sufferings are not worth comparing with the glory that will be revealed in us.

There are no real fairy tales. Wonderful love stories, yes--but no fairy tales. Every real relationship will have difficulties, challenges, and heartaches. But in a healthy relationship, they are far outweighed by the treasure of giving your life to someone who loves you more than he loves himself. You have that opportunity in your relationship with Jesus. It will not be a fairy tale, but it will also not be over when we close the book or the credits roll, and it will be far more amazing because it is real.

CHAPTER 9:
Going Deeper

List lie #1:

_____
_____
_____

Truth with which to fight this lie:

_____
_____
_____
_____

List lie #2:

_____
_____
_____

Truth with which to fight this lie:

_____

_____

_____

List lie #3:

_____

_____

_____

_____

Truth with which to fight this lie:

_____

_____

_____

List lie #4:

_____

_____

_____

_____

Truth with which to fight this lie:

_____

_____

_____

List lie #5:

_____

_____

_____

_____

Truth with which to fight this lie:

_____

_____

_____

List lie #6:

_____

_____

_____

Truth with which to fight this lie:

_____

_____

_____

List lie #7:

_____

_____

_____

Truth with which to fight this lie:

_____

_____

_____

Notes / Thoughts / Prayer

_____

_____

_____

_____

_____

CHAPTER 9: THE FAIRY TALE

Section 3:
The Marriage

Ephesians 5:32 NIV

32 This is a profound mystery — but I am talking about Christ and the church.

After all the waiting and all the advice, we are finally getting married! We have swooned through the courtship, groaned through all the perversions, compared all of that to the amazing relationship God wants to have with us, and now finally we've come to the day for which we've longed.

In this final section we will look at the wonderful and mysterious relationship that occurs in a healthy marriage and how that relationship is really about the relationship between Christ and the church, His bride (Ephesians 5:32-33). It is an incredible thing that God has given us an earthly example to help explain how He feels about us. In spite of the fact that in that heavenly relationship one spouse is always perfect, our earthly marriage can still be a tangible representation of our love affair with Jesus Christ.

We will explore the challenges, the frustrations, the overwhelming love, the fiery passion, the joy and silliness, and even the disappointments and heartaches that come in any marriage. Marriage is a journey. It is a growing organism that must be nurtured and guarded as a precious, delicate treasure. It is a priceless gift, and cared for properly, it will only prove to make us more hungry for a deeper relationship with our Lord.

But first, we must get married. . . .

Love's purpose is to completely give
oneself to another in order to see that
person come fully into his or her destiny.

CHAPTER 10:
The Wedding!

"A man will leave his father and mother and be united to his wife."

Yay! It's finally here! The day we have dreamed of, planned for, and fasted dessert for! We're getting married! We've spent all the endless hours of work and a budget that could have been a down payment on a house for this one single event. But it is absolutely a worthwhile investment. This day is the beginning of a brand new life for us, a whole new identity that we will grow into for the rest of our lives. We are no longer separate entities, but we are now a permanent team. Our destinies are no longer a solo adventure but are now inextricably entwined with one another's. This is a monumental day.

I realize for many of us, even thinking about a wedding day may bring painful memories of great heartache and disappointment in our lives. However, as we look at what God would have for us in a marriage, ask Him to clear away the pain and disillusionment from earthly relationships that fell short of His plan, so that we can embrace the intimacy He longs to have with us. In essence, don't make God pay for others' mistakes. God was not the one who hurt you. He has never and will never lie to you, be unfaithful to you, take you for granted, or abandon you.

Listen to His words. Listen to His heart. Today He longs to take you for His bride, and He has been waiting since before the foundation of the world. He has paid all the expenses for this wedding. He has paid a price you could never comprehend just to see you walk down that aisle. He is risking everything on the chance that you won't reject Him, and He may have the chance to spend the life with you of which He has always dreamed.

It's unlike any commitment you have ever made, and it should be made with a reverent fear, but it is also the most glorious, joyful, mysterious celebration of which you will ever be a part. Welcome to "The Wedding"!

You must understand that when we speak of a marriage with Jesus, it is an "already, but not yet" situation. Although our relationship with Him is to be the most wonderful of marriages, the Bible speaks clearly of "the wedding day" when Jesus will return for His bride and take us home to heaven with Him, and we will celebrate with the most elaborate wedding feast ever imagined. But for the sake of our study we will look at the marriage already in progress, knowing that someday soon we will experience it with Him face to face.

Many parts of the wedding ceremony itself mirror our experience with Christ. Think of the day you made your commitment to Him: most likely you were at church, with friends and family gathered by. There may have even been a few people at the ceremony who were opposed to the union — although as in most wedding ceremonies, no one voiced their objections verbally. Before you walked down that aisle you had done a lot of thinking about this; it was not a spontaneous decision. You had weighed out how you thought your life with this Man would be. You no doubt had numerous questions racing through your thoughts: Am I ready for such a commitment? Am I ready to lose my autonomy? Is He really as wonderful as He appears? What if He doesn't stay that way? What if He breaks my heart? Do we have the same dreams? Does He want children? Does my family approve of Him? Will we be financially stable? And foremost in your mind: Will I be happy?

After hours of thinking through all these issues, you decided this is what you really wanted, and that to spend your life with Him would be worth working through any difficulties the two of you may have.

So you walk down the aisle. All eyes are on you. You pray that you won't fall or do anything to look stupid. You wonder what all these people are thinking as they look at you, but all of that disappears when you catch sight of Him waiting for you at the altar.

He has been looking forward to this day forever. The details of the wedding weren't really that important to Him, but He loves to make you happy and see the excitement on your face as you plan for the big day. All that really matters to Him is you. You are the center of His world. He has told many people that you stole His heart with that first glance (Song of Songs 4:9). To Him you are absolutely flawless and there is no one more beautiful (Song of Songs 4:7, 5:2, and 5:9). He is so overwhelmed with love for you, it is like an unquenchable fire burning in Him (Song of Songs 8:6). He is excited for the ceremony, but His real focus is on finally being alone with you and making you His wife.

Once you take that endlessly long walk down the aisle, the seriousness of this occasion really sinks in. You are standing before the pastor, who is the very representation of the authority of God, and he is explaining to you the true meaning of what you've come to do, and asking you about the commitment you are making to This Man. It almost seems surreal, and yet is the most pivotal moment in your life.

What are those things the pastor talks about? What is this mysterious thing called marriage really about? Ephesians 5:2 says that when Christ speaks of the relationship between a man and wife, He is truly speaking of the mystery of Christ and the Church. We have spoken of this many times, but our earthly marriage is to be a mirror of our relationship with Christ. What is a healthy marriage built on? What is the purpose of this miraculous union? Let's begin in Ephesians chapter 5:21.

Ephesians 5:21-32 NIV
21 Submit to one another out of reverence for Christ.
22 Wives, submit to your husbands as to the Lord. 23 For the husband is the head of the wife as Christ is the head of the church, his body, of which he is the Savior. 24 Now as the church submits to Christ, so also wives should submit to their husbands in everything.
25 Husbands, love your wives, just as Christ loved the church and gave himself up for her 26 to make her holy, cleansing her by the washing with water through the word, 27 and to present her to himself as a radiant church, without stain or wrinkle or any other blemish, but holy and blameless. 28 In this same way, husbands ought to love their wives as their own bodies. He who loves his wife loves himself. 29 After all, no one ever hated his own body, but he feeds and cares for it, just as Christ does the church — 30 for we are members of his body. 31 "For this reason a man will leave his father and mother and be united to his wife, and the two will become one flesh." 32 This is a profound mystery — but I am talking about Christ and the church. 33 However, each one of you also must love his wife as he loves himself, and the wife must respect her husband.

Marriages like this don't exist apart from God. What kind of love does it take to have a marriage like this? 1 Corinthians 13 describes it like this:

1 Corinthians 13:4-13 NIV

4 Love is patient, love is kind. It does not envy, it does not boast, it is not proud. 5 It is not rude, it is not self-seeking, it is not easily angered, it keeps no record of wrongs. 6 Love does not delight in evil but rejoices with the truth. 7 It always protects, always trusts, always hopes, always perseveres. 8 Love never fails. But where there are prophecies, they will cease; where there are tongues, they will be stilled; where there is knowledge, it will pass away. 9 For we know in part and we prophesy in part, 10 but when perfection comes, the imperfect disappears. 11 When I was a child, I talked like a child, I thought like a child, I reasoned like a child. When I became a man, I put childish ways behind me. 12 Now we see but a poor reflection as in a mirror; then we shall see face to face. Now I know in part; then I shall know fully, even as I am fully known.

13 And now these three remain: faith, hope and love. But the greatest of these is love.

This kind of love serves a completely different purpose than the love the world gives. This love's purpose is to completely give oneself to another in order to see that person come fully into his or her destiny. The satisfaction does not come from having one's own way, but from seeing the person you adore become the person God meant for him or her to be. It is a love that reaches to the deepest levels of trust and intimacy. It is a love that forgives completely, when all logic would say that is impossible. It is a love that can see a person prophetically—the way God sees them—instead of the reality of the way they are right now. It is an "agape" love. Agape is a Greek word that means absolutely unconditional. It never ends. Romans 8 says it like this:

Romans 8:35-39 NIV

35 Who shall separate us from the love of Christ? Shall trouble or hardship or persecution or famine or nakedness or danger or sword? 36 As it is written:

"For your sake we face death all day long;
we are considered as sheep to be slaughtered."

37 No, in all these things we are more than conquerors through him who loved us. 38 For I am convinced that neither death nor life, neither angels nor demons, neither the present nor the future, nor any powers, 39 neither height nor depth, nor anything else in all creation, will be able to separate us from the love of God that is in Christ Jesus our Lord.

Nothing can break this marriage up, unless you walk away from it.

The greatest symbol of this love in an earthly marriage is a wedding ring. The greatest symbol of this amazing love in our marriage to Jesus Christ is the cross. The cross was the place of complete sacrifice. It was the place where Jesus showed us a love so great that He would be tortured and killed for His bride. The cross was the place where He gave absolutely everything on the slim chance that His love would win our hearts and we would fall in love with Him. The Bible says we love Him because He first loved us. (1John 4:19) He took on Himself all of our sin and shame and was ridiculed and mocked just for the chance that we would say, "I do." It was the greatest commitment anyone has ever made. It was a covenant unto death. And it was all for me.

The Bible says that before Christ was crucified He had dinner with His disciples and during that dinner He made a covenant with them. We call it communion. It is a symbolic action that signifies the love that Christ has for us and the covenant He has made with us. Jesus instructed us to repeat it often as a reminder until He comes back for us and we are with Him face to face. In this covenant everything we needed was provided for by His death. We are given forgiveness for our sins, healing for our body, mind, and spirit, intimacy with God, and eternal life. His very own blood sealed this covenant. What an amazing husband Jesus is to us.

What is promised in a marriage where this kind of love exists? We have talked about the seriousness of a covenant. What does the covenant of marriage entail? We are very familiar with the traditional wedding vows, and they really are a God-based covenant. The same way in which we take our spouse is the way in which Jesus longs for us to take Him. As you read these vows, take them as a covenant promise in your marriage to Jesus. This is what Jesus has promised you:

I, Jesus, take you to be my lawfully-wedded wife, to have and to hold from this day forward, for richer, for poorer, in sickness and in health, for better and for worse. I will honor you,   love you, and always be with you. I will make you spotless and holy, protect and guide you, lay down my very life for you, 'til death brings us face to face.

Can you make the same vows to Him?

I, _____, take you, Jesus as my lawfully-wedded husband, to have and hold from this day forward, for richer, for poorer, in sickness and in health, for better and for worse. I promise to love you and honor you. I will forsake all others and cling only to you. I will submit to you in obedience, so that I may become a pure, spotless bride by the washing of your blood. I pledge my life completely to you, until death brings us face to face.

The favorite moment of the wedding is the kiss. It is a symbolic sealing of the covenant just made and also a symbol of the intimacy and oneness that is about to take place between this new husband and wife. A kiss is a sign of acceptance, love, and favor. The miracle of being made one and all the symbolism that goes with that is another chapter in itself. But once the kiss occurs the celebration breaks out! It's a celebration of new life, new dreams, new purpose. The Bible says that two are better than one, and that if one can put a thousand to flight, then two can put ten thousand to flight (Deuteronomy 32:30)!

Congratulations on your wedding! May this marriage be everything you've ever dreamed. May you grow more deeply in love each day. May your intimacy intensify on every level: body, soul, and spirit. You have definitely found the perfect mate. Never take Him for granted. Blessings on the adventure that awaits you!

CHAPTER 10:
Going Deeper

1. Marriage with Jesus is an "_____" circumstance.

2. What does Jesus think of His bride (YOU!)?
   a. You _____ His heart with one _____ from your eyes. Song of Songs _____ (scripture reference).
   b. You are absolutely _____ Song of Songs _____ (scripture reference).
   c. You are the most _____ woman in the world. Song of Songs _____ (scripture reference).
   d. His love is like an _____ fire. Song of Songs _____ (scripture reference).

3. Ephesians chapter five gives a short overview of a healthy marriage, but it says that really when God speaks of the two becoming one, He is speaking of what? _____.

4.   The love described in 1 Corinthians 13 is the Greek word _____.
      It means love that is absolutely _____.

5.   This love does not derive its satisfaction from having its own way, but
      from seeing the person it adores become fully the person _____.

6.   This love sees a person the way   _____.

7.   Is their a way to be separated from the love of God? _____.

8.   Much like a wedding ring, the _____ is Christ's symbol
      He gave us of the ultimate sacrifice and commitment.

9.   We love because Christ _____loved us. 1 John 4:19.

10.   Communion symbolizes the _____covenant Jesus made with us.

11.   Four things we are given through this covenant are:
      a. _____
      _____
      _____
      b. _____
      _____
      _____

      c. _____
      _____
      _____
      d. _____
      _____
      _____

Let's make this our vow to Him:

I, _____, take you, Jesus, as my lawfully-wedded husband, to have and hold from this day forward, for richer, for poorer, in sickness and in health, for better and for worse. I promise to love you and honor you. I will forsake all others and cling only to you. I will submit to you in obedience, so that I may become a pure, spotless bride by the washing of your blood. I pledge my life completely to you, until death brings us face to face.

Congratulations and great blessings on your wedding day!

Notes / Thoughts / Prayer

_____
_____
_____
_____
_____
_____
_____
_____
_____
_____
_____
_____
_____
_____
_____
_____
_____
_____
_____

The depth of your intimacy with
Him is completely dependent on your
willingness to accept it.

CHAPTER 11:
The Honeymoon

"The two shall become one."

There are many preconceived ideas about the honeymoon. We are led to believe it will be absolutely perfect. We picture ourselves taking long walks on the beach, enjoying candlelit dinners with soft music in the background, snuggling in front of a fireplace, and soaking in a bubble-filled Jacuzzi. We see ourselves giggling together, whispering sweet nothings to each other, and spending countless hours being intimate with the love of our life. It is heaven on earth, now that we have finally become one with that perfect soul mate.

Sadly, our secular culture would tell you that it's all about the fairy tale, that it's all about the sexual passion. They've reduced it to the high that occurs with orgasm, they advertise "secrets" to increase sexual pleasure, and the pleasure of that act has been cheapened until it has to be enhanced with "toys", "fantasies", or "role playing" to achieve that thrill the next time. Because sex in the world is not based upon God's principles, it becomes shallow and boring and we're taught that it's time to move on to the next relationship.

Rarely does anyone wait to have sex until after the wedding. It is not understood as holy, as part of the covenant, a prophetic symbol of the intimate relationship that occurs between Christ and His bride. They do not understand at all the true significance of the sexual relationship between a husband and wife.

It is an amazing time. There is that incredible miracle of the "two becoming one" (Genesis 2:24), a wonderfully mysterious physical act that is, in reality, a prophetic symbol of what happens spiritually between a husband and wife. It is not only physically the most intimate act that can happen between two people, but it is also meant to be spiritually the most intimate bond two people can have; you are no longer two, but one (Mark 10:8). It is called "consummating" your marriage. It is a consuming of one into the other. It is a complete surrender of one to the other, the greatest act of trust and vulnerability. In a covenant relationship blessed by God, there is complete openness without shame — because the two are one (Genesis 2:25).

Let's look at the intimate relationship between a man and woman the way God does: what does it mean to Him, what did He intend for it to teach us? Even during the wedding we see His symbolism: the bride is dressed in white; she is pure, spotless, consecrated to her husband. Her heart is purely his and her body is reserved for his pleasure. The same is true of the groom. He is set apart for his bride, pure himself, awaiting the time when he can rejoice in the "wife of his youth."

We have talked often of the significance of a blood covenant. Even on the wedding night this comes into play. The blood that is spilled with the breaking of the bride's hymen when she is joined to her groom is representative of a blood covenant. With the active lifestyle of women today, and the much later ages at which we get married, this sign does not occur consistently, but in Jewish culture it was considered a vital sign of virginity for the bride. The sheets were even checked after the wedding night to insure her purity, and if there was no sign of blood, the groom could break the marriage on the grounds that she was not a virgin. It was not a twisted thought in God's mind; it was to give us an understanding of how sacred this physical relationship is; the bride was sealed, set apart for her groom (Ephesians 4:30).

How about beyond the wedding night? What about beyond the initial shyness and newness of the honeymoon? What is the significance of the act itself? Is it solely for the practical purpose of reproduction? Is it a demeaning, necessary evil? Is passion in a Christian marriage inappropriate? Unfortunately, there are those who teach this, and it has only served to create sick, dysfunctional, miserable marriages in the church today. So what was God thinking when He thought this up? If you consider it literally, it is a rather bizarre practice. Yet it is not only physically amazing and wonderful, but spiritually incredible when we really understand what God is showing us through it.

As we touched on earlier, sex is the most intimate physical act that can occur between a man and woman. Because it is symbolic of our relationship with Christ Himself, it is meant to occur only inside of marriage. Ephesians 5:32 tells us that when God speaks of the mystery of a relationship between a husband and wife, He is also speaking of the awesome mystery of the relationship between Christ and the church. Sex experienced outside of marriage is sin not because God is a prude and wants to limit our fun, but because it desecrates the precious thing God created it to be. It takes something holy (set apart, consecrated) and makes it common and misused. It becomes a flippant, selfish thrill, not a prophetic, powerful, and intimate act. Sex outside of marriage will never match the worth, passion, and spiritual depth that sex in a covenant marriage does.

What does the Bible say about the purpose of our body? In general, for every believer, our bodies are the temple of the Holy Spirit, the very dwelling place of the presence of God. For some reason, God has chosen to trust His glory to fleshly bodies, so that the foolish things may be used to shame the wise (1 Corinthians 1:27). Our bodies are meant to be used for holy purposes, not perverse, shallow, or selfish ones.

Romans 6:12-14 NIV

12 Therefore do not let sin reign in your mortal body so that you obey its evil desires. 13 Do not offer the parts of your body to sin, as instruments of wickedness, but rather offer yourselves to God, as those who have been brought from death to life; and offer the parts of your body to him as instruments of righteousness. 14 For sin shall not be your master, because you are not under law, but under grace.

Although the world would tell us it is no big deal to have sex with someone outside of marriage, even that it is prudish not to, the Bible clearly tells us the opposite.

1 Corinthians 6:13-17 NIV

13 The body is not meant for sexual immorality, but for the Lord, and the Lord for the body . 14 By his power God raised the Lord from the dead, and he will raise us also. 15 Do you not know that your bodies are members of Christ himself? Shall I then take the members of Christ and unite them with a prostitute? Never! 16 Do you not know that he who unites himself with a prostitute is one with her in body ? For it is said, "The two will become one flesh." 17 But he who unites himself with the Lord is one with him in spirit.

A simple but powerful illustration of the importance of exclusivity in a marriage is a piece of adhesive tape. When you initially adhere a piece of tape to something the bond is very secure, but if you were to peel that tape off and re-adhere it to something else, you would find the bond not as strong. Every time you repeated that action, the tape would become less and less "sticky." Sex creates a spiritual bond between two people. When that bond is torn apart, and then we try to make that same spiritual "adherence" to someone else, we will find it more difficult to do, and with each successive partner, it becomes more and more difficult, until soon, there is no real bond at all.

God's word continues:

1 Corinthians 6:18-20 NIV
18 Flee from sexual immorality. All other sins a man commits are outside his body, but he who sins sexually sins against his own body . 19 Do you not know that your body is a temple of the Holy Spirit, who is in you, whom you have received from God? You are not your own; 20 you were bought at a price. Therefore honor God with your body.

We are to not only refrain from sexual immorality, but we are to honor God with our bodies. We are to bring Him glory, draw attention to His greatness, goodness, and holiness.

In a marriage we have even further instruction as to God's desire for our bodies.

1 Corinthians 7:3-5 NIV
3 The husband should fulfill his marital duty to his wife, and likewise the wife to her husband. 4 The wife's body does not belong to her alone but also to her husband. In the same way, the husband's body does not belong to him alone but also to his wife. 5 Do not deprive each other except by mutual consent and for a time, so that you may devote yourselves to prayer. Then come together again so that Satan will not tempt you because of your lack of self-control.

One's body belongs to one's spouse! I like that! You need to understand that in all that is done in marriage, honor is the highest principle. If something you do is dishonoring to your spouse, then it is sin. That is not what we are dealing with here. The point is that we are one. We belong to each other, and sex is a God-thought-of, God-ordained idea! He tells us not to neglect it. When you read this passage, written by Paul, he gives you his own opinion on the matter, but Paul had the gift of celibacy and was perfectly content without a wife. That was a God-given gift for Paul, but it's certainly not for most people, and thank goodness, or there would be no human race!

The very act of sex itself is meant to be one of total surrender in love. It is not meant to be taken by force. The full pleasure of it cannot even occur outside of the context of surrender. When you look at the psychological and emotional differences between a man and a woman that affect their physiological responses, it's obvious that God meant for sex to happen in a giving, loving context. Generally for men, intimacy is sex. For women it is talking, and connecting emotionally. For a man, climax is a physical response, easily achieved, but in order for his wife to truly be "one" with him, he must sacrifice that immediate gratification in order to give himself for her, to woo her and to romance her, so that in the end there is an even greater reward. And although sex is certainly immensely pleasurable for women also, we are called to give ourselves to our husbands physically in a way that meets their needs, even though at times we may be content to just cuddle. I think the best description I've heard is that men are like microwaves and women are like crock pots. The pleasure of sex is not just about the physical sensation, but about really enjoying pleasing your spouse and giving yourself for them, and to them, just as Christ set the example for us.

Christ romances us the same way. Just as physical intimacy cannot be forced, neither can spiritual intimacy. One can "go through the motions" of either act, but it doesn't insure intimacy. Rape is not an intimate event. Prostitution is not an intimate event. Sexual abuse is not an intimate event. Although they all may include sexual intercourse, none contains the absolutely vital elements necessary for intimacy. Intimacy is a completely voluntary emotion. The vulnerability, trust, and desire that must be present are also voluntary. If they are forced, then by very nature, it is not intimacy; it is rape. Christ will not spiritually "rape" you to achieve a false intimacy with you. The depth of your intimacy with Him is completely dependent on your willingness to accept it. You are as close to Christ as you want to be. It is totally up to you, because He is ever-waiting for as intimate a relationship as you will allow. We must also understand that just going through the motions like a spiritual "prostitute" does not count as intimacy. We can sing, lift our hands, dance, cry, give in the offering, be at every church event, and read our Bible every day, but those can all just be an appearance of intimacy when there is no reality of it. It's all about relationship, not actions. The actions will follow naturally when the relationship is established, but actions will not create an intimate bond.

Just as your relationship with Christ grows richer and deeper over time, so should your relationship with your spouse. This is true not only in everyday life, but physically as well. As you mature in your understanding of the correlation between your earthly marriage and your marriage to Christ, the preciousness and sacredness of your physical relationship becomes more real. The awkwardness is gone, the giving increases, the amazement of the gift God has given you in your spouse becomes even more real. It doesn't become old or boring. It is communion with one another. It is the only part of your spouse that you will never have to share with anyone else. It is your gift alone. It's a joyful time, a fun time. It's not meant to be a chore. With all the demands of daily life, it is a precious time for just the two of you to share with each other what no one else can have. That is why the wound is almost impossible to heal when that trust has been broken; it is irreparable, except for the grace of God.

The other significant thing that comes from this incredible intimacy is fruitfulness. We have many examples in the Bible of fruitfulness being considered a blessing (Leviticus 26:9) and unfruitfulness being a curse (Genesis 30:2). The first command man and woman were given was to be fruitful and multiply (Genesis 1:28). Jesus even cursed the fig tree because it wasn't fruitful (Matthew 21:19). Let's lay aside all the arguments for and against birth control for right now so that we can catch the spiritual point of this. Let's go back in time when the only birth control was abstinence during the fertile time of the woman's cycle. Of course you know what we call people that use that method: parents! Oh, God knows how to bless us in spite of ourselves! The point being this: in a normal, healthy relationship, when everything is functioning properly, the expected outcome is a pregnancy. That's how God designed us. It is His blessing on our union and our lives. If a pregnancy doesn't occur, then something is wrong. It could come from a multitude of different sources, and it's not the same for each couple, but something is wrong. The same is true of our marriage to Christ. When the relationship is healthy, it is productive, it is fruitful; you'll become pregnant and give birth in a spiritual sense! That is God's plan for you and it is His blessing on your union with Jesus and on your life!

My "blanket story" is one of the most profound encounters I've had with God on the subject of intimacy. Just to recap, I was whining to God about an attitude I had that I felt He was unjustly asking me to give up. As I was griping about how much more He expected of me than others, He reminded me of an event that occurred one cold winter night between my husband and me. I had gone to bed before my husband, but because I was very cold, I wrapped myself up in a blanket before crawling between the sheets and pulling the comforter up around me. Because I had already turned the light off before my husband crawled into bed, he was unaware of my cocoon. When he reached over to snuggle up to me, he kept pulling and tugging at the sheets and my personal blanket trying to get to me and was very confused as to why he couldn't "find" me. Finally, with great frustration, he asked, "Whatcha got goin' on here?" Although I got a good laugh at the time, God used it to show me that my attitude was like that blanket. I was cold (angry and hurt), so it was natural to want a blanket (attitude of offense), and God, like my husband, wanted to be intimate with me, but I was making it impossible because of my unwillingness to remove my "blanket." It was the first time I truly realized that God required holiness of me, not just because He is holy, but because He desperately wants to be intimate with me, and intimacy cannot happen with something in the way. Anything that comes between God and me is sin. I may see my sin as a thick comforter, or just a thin sheet, but either one will prevent spiritual intimacy and thus, fruitfulness in my life.

God desires to impregnate us with His destiny for our lives. If we will make ourselves vulnerable to intimacy with Him, He will come and fill us with His seed—His plans and dreams. As we stay in relationship with Him, that seed is implanted in our spiritual womb, and it is nurtured and grows inside us. When the gestation period is over we will give birth to that vision and it will become a reality. Some of us become so overwhelmed by the magnitude of what God has placed in us that we abort the baby for fear that we won't be able to care for it or be a proper parent. Others of us desperately want to be fruitful and have Jesus impregnate us with His dreams for us, but we have wrapped ourselves in blankets of past hurt or dysfunction or fear. And since God will not force us into intimacy or to remove the things we think are keeping us "safe," He patiently waits and all the while we remain barren and confused. The difficulty for many of us who have become pregnant with His purpose is being willing to endure the gestation period required for the "baby" to mature. We feel like it's just taking too long and we try to "deliver" before the baby is ready. The eminent danger with a premature birth is that a premature baby is rarely healthy and strong and may even die soon after birth. Never rush God's gestation period. A true mother will endure anything to ensure the health and safety of her baby, even if it means laying down her very life. Let us be true mothers to the destinies God gives us. The evidence of a healthy life and marriage is fruitfulness. God's plan for our lives is great fruitfulness, but it can only come through intimacy.

The joys and rewards of a marriage to Jesus Christ are unimaginable and never ending. It is a journey full of adventure and blessing. Run into it full force. Open yourself up with complete abandon. You will never regret it.

CHAPTER 11:
Going Deeper

1.   To ensure that sex does not become shallow and boring, it must be based on _____.

2.   The physical relationship between a husband and wife is a _____ symbol of the spiritual relationship between _____ and_____.

3.   Sex is not only the most intimate _____ act that happens between a husband and wife, but also the most intimate _____one.

4.   The most amazing thing that happens, even spiritually, in this union is that _____.

5.   How is the wedding night, that first sexual encounter, a prophetic act?

     _____

     _____

_____

_____

_____

_____

6. Which book in the Bible is dedicated to teaching us that love and sexual passion is GODLY?

    _____

    _____

    _____

    _____

    _____

    _____

    Read it!

7. Sex outside of the covenant of marriage takes something meant to be ___ _____ (consecrated and set apart) and makes it _____ and _____.

8. For every believer, our bodies are the _____ and meant to glorify God. (Romans 6:12-14, 1 Corinthians 6:13-7:1)

9. Specifically for those married, your body belongs to _____ _____. (1 Corinthians 7:3-6)

10. By its very nature, intimacy cannot be_____. It occurs only when it is _____.

11. Three vital elements of intimacy:
    a. _____
    b. _____
    c. _____

12. Christ will never force _____ upon you.

13. Your relationship with Christ is as intimate as _____.

14. Your physical relationship with your spouse is the only thing you will never have to _____ with anyone else. It is your gift alone.

15. The other significant thing that comes from this incredible intimacy is_____.

16. God expects fruitfulness out of _____relationship.

17. God desires to _____ us with His _____ for our lives!

18. Two dangers to our destiny are _____ it and not_____.

Notes / Thoughts / Prayer

_____

_____

_____

_____

_____

_____

_____

_____

_____

_____

_____

_____

_____

_____

_____

_____

_____

We have intimate access to God through the new covenant Jesus made for us.

CHAPTER 12:

Access Through Covenant

"Total surrender grants total access."

In researching for this chapter I found a lot of information on covenants, but none of it really had the complete heart that I feel like God wants us to have concerning our covenant with Him. Although the information was factual, I felt that it fell short of the new covenant of which God was speaking in Jeremiah and then again in Hebrews:

Hebrews 8:7-13
[7]For if there had been nothing wrong with that first covenant, no place would have been sought for another. [8]But God found fault with the people and said,

"The time is coming, declares the Lord, when I will make a new covenant with
the house of Israel
and with the house of Judah.
[9]It will not be like the covenant
I made with their forefathers
when I took them by the hand
to lead them out of Egypt,
because they did not remain faithful to my covenant,
and I turned away from them, declares the Lord.

[10]This is the covenant I will make with the house of Israel

after that time, declares the Lord.
I will put my laws in their minds
and write them on their hearts.
I will be their God,
and they will be my people.

[11]*No longer will a man teach his neighbor,*
or a man his brother, saying, 'Know the Lord,'
because they will all know me,
from the least of them to the greatest.

[12]*For I will forgive their wickedness*
and will remember their sins no more."[c]
[13]*By calling this covenant "new," he has made the first*
one obsolete; and what is obsolete and aging will soon
disappear.

The entire book of Hebrews is about how Jesus is better:

• He's better than the angels (Chapter 1).
• He's better than Moses and the prophets (Chapter 3).
• He brings a better rest (Chapter 4).
• He's a better high priest (Chapters 4, 5, and 7).
• He brings a better covenant (Chapter 8).
• His blood is better (Chapter 9).
• His sacrifice is better (Chapters 9 and 10).

Everything about Jesus was better. Hebrews talks about how the old covenant was imperfect. It served a purpose because it gave us a picture of things to come. It was based on the law although the essence of God's heart is freedom and grace, not the law.

Most times in church circles when we teach on covenant it is through "law-based lenses." We talk about the requirements and regulations of covenant but disregard the benefits thereof. God has been teaching me over the past few years about access through covenant, through relationship, if you will. The purpose of covenant for God was not to give us a set of rules or to control us but to bless us and be in an everlasting relationship with us. He is not a distant God. He is a God who, in spite of being so much greater than us, created us to be intimate with Him. That's the whole purpose of the new covenant!

If you study the Jewish temple at the time of Christ you'll see that there was an extremely heavy, multi-layered curtain, or veil, as they called it, between the outer court-- where priests were allowed to enter on a regular basis-- and the inner court, or Holy of Holies--where the high priest entered only once a year to make the sacrifice for the atonement of sins. This curtain was 60' tall, 30' wide and 3" thick. It signified the separation of man from the very presence of God. At the moment of Jesus' death on the cross, God supernaturally tore the curtain in half, beginning at the top and moving to the bottom. It was an incredible picture of what Jesus' death on the cross did in God's eyes---it gave us personal access to the very presence of God! That's God's heart! That was God's idea from the beginning. Remember how He walked every evening in the Garden of Eden with Adam and Eve? He loves to be with us. He wants friends, not servants; a bride, not a slave. The covenant that Christ made on the cross gives us that relationship back. It gives us intimate access as His bride.

Let's look at the difference in access that a bride has to her husband compared with others around him. What are some benefits the Bride of Christ has that others don't have?

- I have His name (Revelation 2:17).
- All that He has is mine (Luke 15:31, Luke 12:32).
- He has given me His life (John 3:16).
- He tells me the secrets of His heart (1 Corinthians 4:1).
- I am His and He is mine (Song of Songs 2:16).
- I have access to Him that others don't (Ephesians 2:14).
- He lives His life for my benefit (Philippians 2).
- He loves to be with me (Song of Songs---the entire book!).
- It is a life-long relationship (Psalm 105:10).
- He protects me (Psalm 91:1).
- I am the apple of His eye (Psalm 17:8).
- He provides for me (Philippians 4:19).
- I am cherished and adored (Song of Songs---again, the entire book!).
- I live in a place of intimacy with Him that produces fruit (John 15:4).
- As I am continually intimate with Him, my DNA even changes to be like His (2 Corinthians 3:18).

WOW! That's a whole lot better than being a slave with a bunch of rules! Mike Bickle, founder of the International House of Prayer, has a saying, "There are workers and there are lovers, and lovers get way more done than do workers." When I am in love I don't need a set of rules to make me behave or honor my husband. My heart is fully his, and it is my joy to please him and bless him. I want to be with him. I don't want to hurt him. My relationship with him is something I pursue, not something I am obligated to keep. Even when things are difficult I think it worth the price to have him in my life and be his wife.

We have intimate access to God through the new covenant Jesus has made for us. He has moved us from being servants to being friends. We have become His very bride, the one He has CHOSEN to spend eternity with! He has invited us to more than just following rules handed out from a distant God who is concerned only about our doing what is right and spends His days counting our mistakes. He is far more concerned about US, our dreams, hurts, and accomplishments than He is about what we do wrong. He has already paid for all our mistakes by His death---they are all covered. Now He is pouring into our purpose as His children and heirs to His kingdom. It's such a different ballgame! We have become partners with Him—how amazing is that, that we are God's partners?

Our lives move from being about what we do to being about who we are. Our accomplishments come out of WHO we are, not what we do. It's just a completely different way to live. My worth isn't based on what I accomplish; it's based on what was paid for me---and that amount was priceless! All striving is gone. In the natural, I don't worry that if I take a day off my husband might not love me. I don't worry that if I go without makeup or gain 10 (or even 100) pounds he will feel any differently about me. He didn't marry me because of my degree or my money. In my relationship with God the same is true. God doesn't love me because of what I do for Him, and if I make a mistake or even rebel, His love for me remains the same. I have such a place of security and unconditional love that I flourish and become fully who I was created to be.

What different lives we would live if we truly believed who we are and all that God desires for us. We live far beneath the level at which He has paid for us to live. Wouldn't it be strange for a wife to live as her husband's servant? To be invited to his bed night after night but insist on living over the garage in the servants' quarters instead? To spend only what is equal to minimum wage when all the while she is a signatory on an endless bank account? To serve him dinner but never sit and talk with him as they ate? To address him as "Mr. So and So" instead of "my Beloved?" For both of them to long for children but for her never to be intimate enough with her husband to conceive one? That would all be so ridiculously tragic, yet we live our lives as the bride of Christ that way. All that is His, He has made ours--all resources, healing, joy, kingdom authority, and abundant life above anything we could dream or imagine!

It's all ours because we are His bride and we have His name. I pray that somehow God would take this truth from being information in our heads to being revelation in our hearts! He invites us to such intimate access to Him----come in!

CHAPTER 12:
Going Deeper

1. God desires a covenant that is written on our _____.
    (Hebrews 8: 8-13)

2. In the book of Hebrews it shows Jesus was better in what ways?

    Chapter 1:

    _____
    _____
    _____
    _____

    Chapter 3:

    _____
    _____
    _____

Chapters 4, 5, and 7:

_____

_____

_____

_____

Chapter 8:

_____

_____

_____

_____

Chapter 9 and 10:

_____

_____

_____

_____

3. We were created to be _____ with God.

4. What was torn when Jesus died?

    _____

5. What was the significance of that?

    _____

    _____

6. What advantages do I have by being Christ's bride?

    •   I have His _____. (Revelation 2:17)
    •   All that He has is _____. (Luke 15:31, Luke 12:32)
    •   He has given me His _____. (John 3:16)

- He tells me the _____ of His heart. (1 Corinthians 4:1)
- I am _____ and He is _____. (Song of Solomon 2:16)
- I have _____ to Him that others don't. (Ephesians 2:14)
- He lives His life for my _____. (Philippians 2)
- He loves to _____. (Song of Solomon--THE WHOLE BOOK!)
- It is a _____ relationship. (Psalm 105:10)
- He _____ me. (Psalm 91:1)
- I am the _____of His eye. (Psalm 17:8)
- He _____ for me. (Philippians 4:19)
- I am _____ and _____. (Song of Solomon — WHOLE BOOK!)
- I live in a place of intimacy with Him that produces _____. (John 15:4)
- As I am continually intimate with Him my _____ Even changes to be like His. (2 Corinthians 3:18)

7. We are no longer _____, but _____. (John 15:15)

8. God rejoices in who we _____, not what we _____.

"There are workers and there are lovers;
and lovers get more done than workers."
Mike Bickle.

ENJOY BEING THE BRIDE!

Notes / Thoughts / Prayer

_____

_____

_____

Marriage is like a river in which the water flows and changes according to its journey, but the banks which hold it are stable and secure, guiding it safely to its destination.

CHAPTER 13:

A Healthy Marriage

"Love never fails."

We've spent a lot of time talking about the courtship and then the dysfunctions possible in a relationship. Now that we've discussed all the things that fall short of God's plan for us, let's talk about the blessings He has planned for us in a healthy, godly marriage! The world hardly knows what one looks like, and if they even have an idea of what one is, they feel it's just an unreachable goal, a fairy tale with no hope of becoming a reality. How sad, when God has planned for marriage to be the very mirror in which we see our relationship with Christ!

There are many facets to a healthy marriage. Marriage is like a river in which the water flows and changes according to its journey, but the banks which hold it are stable and secure, guiding it safely to its destination. Marriage goes through different seasons, but they are all held in God's hand.

The most widely held definition of love is quite different than God's definition of love. God commands us to love each other; to God, love is something we can choose to do, not just feel. This is incomprehensible to those who believe one falls in and out of love, something quite beyond one's control. So to make God's definition of love more understandable and achievable, let's call it honor.

The highest requirement of a healthy marriage is honor. It is like the spine that holds everything else up. If you truly honor each other, all other issues can be worked out. At first thought, one may think a romantic love should be the basis; however, love may not always exist in a marriage, especially the overwhelming, passionate love we all dream of for our marriages. This feeling may have existed at one time, or it may be a case in which it has never been. Until recent history, arranged marriages were the norm. Romantic love was rarely the basis for putting a couple together. If a marriage could be successful only when romantic love was involved, then the large majority of marriages were failures to begin with. Fortunately, many of those couples understood the principles of a good marriage and made the commitment necessary to see their marriage go from a "good arrangement" to a loving, stable relationship.

Of course, God's desire is that marriage be a passionate, love-filled adventure, a life lived together, pursuing the destiny God has put in the two of you. So how do you achieve that? And how do you keep doing that when it seems impossible? 1 Corinthians 13 is known as the "Love Chapter." Sounds like an idea straight out of the 50's, but it's actually quite the opposite. This chapter describes the vertebrae that make up the spine called honor, and each vertebra needs to be in place in order for the marriage to be strong, stable, and growing in love.

1 Corinthians 13:4-8 NIV
4 Love is patient, love is kind. It does not envy, it does not boast, it is not proud.
5 It is not rude, it is not self-seeking, it is not easily angered, it keeps no record
of wrongs. 6 Love does not delight in evil but rejoices with the truth. 7 It always
protects, always trusts, always hopes, always perseveres. 8 Love never fails.

Wow! I think this is the hardest part of the Bible to obey, because it's not just a bunch of do's and don'ts; it cuts to our heart, our very motives. No matter how well we may fake it on the outside, it's not truly love---or honor---unless our motives are pure. I do want to make it clear that love is a choice. God doesn't command us to do something that can't be done. We choose to love. The feeling doesn't have to be there, but it will eventually follow. Loving someone the way Christ commands us to requires that we continually check our motives and make a commitment to love them no matter what may happen or how that person may act. Loving as Christ loves involves daily laying down our lives for the benefit of those we love. There is no picking and choosing which disciplines of love we think are reasonable for us to follow. They are all equally important and equally commanded.

This kind of sacrificial love can flow through us only when God is our source. When we surrender our feelings, our "rights," and our desires to Him, He will give us a grace—an empowerment—to love even the seemingly unlovable. The joy of loving doesn't always spring from how those we love respond to us, but from knowing that we please God's heart. It is in understanding exactly what Matthew 25:40 says, that when we love others we truly love Christ. Although struggling to love our spouse is hopefully the exception, not the rule, this motivation will enable us to be consistent in our love for him or her, regardless of their response.

God has declared throughout the Bible the benefits of being married. It's not just a financial arrangement or merely a cultural norm. He declares that "two are better than one" (Ecclesiastes 4:9-12). God has created man and woman to complement each other. When you become one through the covenant of marriage, not only do you physically and spiritually become one but your destinies become entwined as well. That is not to say that God no longer has an individual plan for your life, but in His sovereign creativity He creates a destiny for the two of you as one! What an encouragement and blessing to have a lifelong teammate pursuing your destiny with you! When one falls, the other picks him or her up; when the enemies attack, you can win against them together! Deuteronomy 32:30 says that one can put a thousand to flight, but two will put ten thousand to flight when God is with them. Check out that multiplication!

In the same way God loves to partner with us to see incredible things happen, He loves to see us partner with each other! The theme of teamwork, or "body life," permeates His word. He gives analogy after analogy of each member of the body doing its part (Ephesians 4:16), of believers being living stones of which the temple is made (1 Peter 2:5), and we are described as an army, a royal priesthood. We're meant to work together!

If you've played sports, you understand how important the individual skills of each player are. When you're five years old and swinging at a ball on a tee, skill isn't that important (being cute is enough). But as you get older teams are looking for those athletes whose skills complete their team. A true athlete understands that you don't want or need twelve quarterbacks on a team. That's a disaster, and your team will never win. Quarterbacks may be more noticeable, but they will spend their careers on their backs if there is no one to block for them. They may be the greatest quarterbacks in the world, but no one will ever know that if they don't have a skilled offensive line and receivers to catch the ball. The winning team is the one whose players pride themselves on the team's victories, the team's strategy, their teammates' accomplishments, and not just their own.

Marriage must be built on the same principle. We're a team! It's not about you or me; it's about us! It's about our being better together than we are apart. It's about God sovereignly bringing two people together who play different positions on the team because He knows that together you're unstoppable! Just like on a sports team, you each have your own skills at which you excel. At times one will be more noticeable, and then at times the other, but the point is that neither succeeds alone. One is the quarterback who throws that incredible pass, and the other is the receiver who leaps high above the opponent to catch it and run it in for the goal. You're both amazing, and when you work together it is such an fulfilling experience. And because it is such a rarity, the world marvels at you and longs to play that way. You mirror the oneness of Jesus and the Father mentioned in John 17:20-23. Christ longed for us to have that kind of unity not only so that our joy might be full, but so the world would see it and know that God loves them just as He loves Jesus Himself.

Although this book is not meant to be a counseling book on relationships, I feel we need to look at some other foundational requirements for a strong, healthy, passionate marriage, because we tend to treat God the same way in which we treat our spouse. A few days ago I sat for over an hour with a beautiful young lady who has been married for around 15 years. As she shared her story and asked my advice on problem after problem in her marriage, it was evident she had been down this list many times, with many pastors. She was looking for a quick fix for a marriage that has been in trouble for years. She also wanted the "fix" to justify her feelings and actions, to show her husband to be the jerk she believes he is, with her as the godly victim which she believes she is. It was such a long, rehearsed list my first response to her was the wise words I've heard my husband tell people many times, "Well, you didn't get into this mess overnight, and you won't get out of it overnight." It was a prime example of the fact that love isn't enough in any marriage. "Love is all you need" ("All You Need is Love," The Beatles, 1967) might have been a great anthem in the sixties, but it wasn't exactly written by stellar examples of a godly or successful marriage.

In order for any marriage to work, "ya gotta have skills"; skills like communication, crisis management, conflict resolution, household management, financial management, and child rearing skills, if applicable. No matter how much you love someone, or how wonderful he or she may be, if you do not have these life skills, there is very little chance that your marriage will survive. Some of us were blessed to have been taught these skills as we were growing up. We saw them modeled by our parents, teachers, pastors, and other adults involved in our lives. They walked us through conflict, discussed the good and bad examples, and gave us sound biblical counsel so that our decisions and responses were based on God's word. Even with the best of upbringings, it is vital that we continue to hone these skills so that all our relationships thrive.

But many of us were not so fortunate. We grew up in crippling dysfunction but perceived it as normal and healthy because we had no other example. We saw the same patterns and cycles lived out daily, not only in our generation, but in our parents'and grandparents'. No one ever acquired the skills, so the cycle was never broken. Divorce, promiscuity, illegitimate pregnancies, abuse, anger, perversion, and addiction were seen as the common way of life. We thought the best we could hope for in life was a fleeting moment of happiness or even a cheap thrill. We had no idea that the dream was attainable, so we settled for a counterfeit instead of all that God has for us.

Many times we do the same thing in our relationship with God. He has so much more for us than what we have settled for. Before He even created us in our mothers' wombs, He ordained our "dream" (Psalm 139:16). Ephesians 3:20 says that God is able to do far above anything we can ask or imagine. Don't fall into the trap of looking at your pastor or someone on TV and thinking that you could never have that kind of relationship with God. Friendship with God is not an elitist thing. We are as close to God as we want to be. James 4:8 says, "Draw near to God and He will draw near to you." Ask God for a new paradigm. Ask Him to show you the real, not the counterfeit. He longs for so much more in this relationship with you than you could ever imagine. He longs for a sweet, intimate, passionate marriage with you that grows stronger and more vibrant each day. Go for the dream!

CHAPTER 13:
Going Deeper

LOVE IS A VERB!

1.	To God love is something you can _____not just _____.

2.	Another word for love is _____.

3.	The highest requirement for a healthy marriage is _____.

4.	Why can't romantic love be the basis for a marriage?

	_____

	_____

	_____

	_____

5.   Which chapter in the Bible is known as the Love Chapter?

_____

6.   What is the reference for God's definition of love?

_____

GOD BELIEVES IN TEAMWORK!

7.   Deuteronomy 32:30 — "One can put a thousand to flight, but two will put _____to flight!"

8.   In Ephesians 4:16 we are parts of a _____. In 1 Peter 2:5 we are _____, parts of a temple.

9.   A winning team is one whose players pride themselves on the _____ victories, the _____ strategy, and their _____ accomplishments, not just their own.

10.   In marriage, it's not about you or me; it's about_____.

11.   Love isn't enough — ya gotta have _____!

12.   List some skills needed for a successful marriage:

_____

_____

_____

_____

_____

_____

Regardless of our background, God has made available to us all that we need to break cycles of dysfunction.

13.   What does James 4:8 assure us of?

_____

_____

_____

_____

_____

_____

14.   To change our lives we need:

_____

_____

_____

_____

_____

_____

"Do not conform any longer to the pattern of this world, but be transformed by the renewing of your mind. Then you will be able to test and approve what God's will is–His good pleasing and perfect will."
Romans 12:1-3 NIV

Notes / Thoughts / Prayer

_____

_____

_____

_____

_____

_____

_____

_____

_____

_____

I think the biggest mistake
most couples make is
underestimating the value of
their marriage.

CHAPTER 14:

Safeguarding Your Marriage

"Relationships require investment."

We talked about the absolute need for marriage skills in the last chapter and briefly mentioned some of those: communication, crisis management, conflict resolution, household management, financial management, and child rearing skills. All of these skills, used wisely, help to safeguard your marriage. We've already said that marriage is not a fairy tale. Love is not all you need. This is a lifelong covenant made before God, with each person promising that, to the absolute best of his or her ability, only death will end the relationship. That's a serious promise. Because He takes it so seriously (and we know He does, since He gave it as a mirror of our relationship with Him), God must see marriage as incredibly valuable, something to be guarded and protected at any cost. Let's use this chapter as an abbreviated training guide for "marriage safeguards."

I think the biggest mistake most couples make is underestimating the value of their marriage. If you don't understand what you have, or even the potential of what you have, most likely you will not guard it well.

I remember speaking at an event once where I was illustrating this point (although in a different context). Before I spoke I put my wedding rings in a crumpled up brown paper bag and during the meal before I spoke, I asked the person next to me if they would mind holding this bag for me. I gave them no details or special instructions, just casually asked them to hold it for me. We finished our lunch, sang some songs, they made some announcements, I was introduced, and proceeded to speak to this crowd about the importance of caring for what God entrusts to us, even though we may not fully understand its value at the time. Finally, at the end of my message, I asked the friend next to me if she still had the bag I had given her, and (much to my tremendous relief) she brought it to me. The crowd was understandably shocked that I had put my wedding rings (which are also a family heirloom) in a bag and just trusted her to watch it without knowing what was inside. (I might add that I didn't tell my husband this brilliant illustration until I got home with them safely, either!) But isn't that what God does with us? He gives us the most amazing, precious gifts in our lives---our parents, our children, our friends, our spouses, our marriages----and just entrusts them to our care hoping we will look beyond the outward packaging to see the priceless jewels inside! Guard well what He gives you. You have no idea the value of what you hold!

What are some steps we can take to guard our marriages? The most common sense, best overall way to safeguard our marriages is to follow the Golden Rule: "Treat others as you would like to be treated." Sounds too simple, huh? We learn that rule when we're toddlers, and yet some of us still struggle to put it into practice. We can be embarrassingly self-centered, worried about how we feel and what we want, what we need and what we think! We can continually put ourselves first and just run over everyone else in the process. There's a huge push currently to follow the maxim that I need to "take care of me." To an extent that's true. In the same way you would care for any of God's creation, yes, take care of yourself. But what if Jesus had put Himself first? This is what the Bible says:

Philippians 2:5-11 NIV
5 Your attitude should be the same as that of Christ Jesus:
6 Who, being in very nature of God, did not consider equality with God something to be grasped,
7 but made himself nothing,
taking the very nature of a servant,
being made in human likeness.
8 And being found in appearance as a man,
he humbled himself and became obedient to death —
even death on a cross!

Wow! That's a little different than the "I'm leaving you because I'm not having my needs met!" crowd, huh? Jesus became a servant. He humbled Himself and served others.

Mark 10:45 NIV

*45 For even the Son of Man did not come to be served, but to serve, and to give
his life as a ransom for many.*

The only One who deserved to be served humbled Himself and became a
servant to us, even to the extent that it cost Him His very life! But how can we be happy
or successful if we don't take care of ourselves? Who's going to look out for us if we
don't look out for ourselves? Let's see what happened with Jesus:

Philippians 2:9-11 NIV
*9 Therefore God exalted him to the highest place
and gave him the name that is above every name,
10 that at the name of Jesus every knee should bow,
in heaven and on earth and under the earth,
11 and every tongue confess that Jesus Christ is Lord,
to the glory of God the Father.*

Whoa! God has such a different economy than we do! In the Kingdom of God,
we humble ourselves and at the proper time, God exalts us (Matthew 23:12)! The first
becomes last, but the last becomes first (Matthew 20:16)! God is well able to cover my
back! He is my defender and the one who insures justice for me. His mercies are new
every morning, and His grace is never ending. I can afford to serve others. I can afford
to serve my spouse. As a matter of fact, I can't afford not to.

Please understand that this kingdom mindset is for everyone in the kingdom--
-men and women. Unfortunately the church has spent years manipulating scripture to
create a disproportionate bride for Jesus.

I laugh when I think about our first church service after my husband and I
married. We were married on Saturday night and drove to a small resort town for our
honeymoon. The next morning we got up and went to church together for the first time
as Mr. and Mrs. Shannon Schreyer. When we arrived at the church they immediately
ushered us into separate Sunday school classrooms, because they were divided by
gender. I'm not sure what the men's teacher was teaching about, but the women's
teacher was teaching from Ephesians chapter 5, all about wives submitting to their
husbands. I thought, "Good grief! This has to be a setup!" It was quite ironic for my
first married church service.

Even then I had the mindset that prevailed in the church: that it's only for
women to submit to men. But to be interpreted correctly all scripture must be taken in
context, and verse 21 of that chapter states first off that we *submit to one another* out of
reverence for Christ. When Christ commanded us to serve and submit, he meant for

us all to do it for each other out of reverence for Christ! When we all follow the Golden Rule there is joy and peace in everything we do. Does it always happen that way? Unfortunately, no, but that is where grace comes in. That is when we lean so heavily on the promise that "I can do all things through Christ who strengthens me" (Philippians 4:13).

Let's get practical about what treating someone else the way we would like to be treated looks like. If you've ever read <u>The Five Love Languages,</u> which is a wonderful book by Gary Smalley, you know that people feel loved and valued in different ways. For instance, my strongest love language is definitely "works of service." I am a Missouri girl; if you want to convince me that you love me---SHOW ME! Help me, do something for me: clean the house, fix my car, repair what's broken, take out the trash, do something for me that I hate doing! I don't need gifts or roses---just pick up your socks!

Now, not everyone has the same "love language," but we each want to be treated in a way that shows respect and honor.

Some of those ways are so basic. Let me give you a quick cheat sheet:

- Love God more than you love me.
- Don't insult me, even if you say it's just a joke.
- Don't raise your voice to me.
- Don't make fun of me.
- Don't embarrass me in front of other people.
- Treat me like a prince/ princess when we're together.
- Look at me when we talk.
- Listen-----really.
- Don't interrupt me.
- Hold my hand.
- Kiss me hello and goodbye.
- Tell me you love me---daily, at the very least.
- Tell me I'm handsome/beautiful.
- Brag about me to your friends, family, and our kids.
- When all is said and done, I need to see that I am more important to you than your family, our kids, your job, money, friends, hobbies, time, etc. Those all matter, but I matter to you the most.
- Remember, I'm not your maid, your mommy, your daddy, a paycheck, a nanny, or your only source of happiness.
- Always sleep in the same bed as I.
- Never go to sleep mad at me.

- Make love with me.
- Call me, text me, and miss me when we're apart.
- Don't forget my birthday and our anniversary.
- Pray with me and for me.
- Don't criticize me to our children or anyone else.
- Believe the best of me.
- Challenge me.
- Encourage me.
- Dream with me.
- Be my biggest fan.
- Make time to be with me.
- Tell me the truth in love.
- Even when I'm not with you, respect me by behaving as though I am.
- Remember we are on the same team, working for the same goal: to fully experience this amazing adventure God has called our destiny.

It's certainly not an all-inclusive list, but good things to remember.

I want to encourage you also to really enjoy your marriage and each other. I don't know if I can adequately describe it, but God wants us to live in rest, not striving. In the midst of all things we need to do to have a good marriage, it's vitally important that we are at ease with each other and confident that what God began, He will guard and complete. When my husband and I first married I went through about three months of being what I would describe as functionally depressed. I absolutely adored my husband and knew there was no one else with whom I wanted to spend my life, but because of the culture in which I was raised and other circumstances, I was terrified I would end up divorced. I was raised in a pastor's home and every man in my family was a pastor. My parents had an amazing marriage and divorce was quite rare, even in our extended family.

Although that should have encouraged me, I was quite fearful that I would be the first one to mess it up! And I couldn't imagine anything worse. To top that off, we had two couples that were close to us become engaged around the same time we had and both of them broke off their engagements before their weddings. I had heard (be it true or not) that most marriages end in the seventh year. I became fixated on whether or not we would make it past that seventh year. In the midst of that, we lived very close to my parents, and although that was such a precious time (my father passed away two years after I married), I had quite a struggle trying to figure out what role I was to play now that I was married. Was I my parents' little girl? My husband's wife? Did I have to get up at four in the morning now like my mom always had? (I could easily stay up until four, but getting up at four was not my bag!)

My husband came from a very different background than my family, so I struggled to know if it was okay for our free time, work schedule, etc. to look different than my family's. Fortunately, my husband was incredibly flexible and loves my family deeply, so he made most of the adjusting. He was very patient with me. To top that off, people in our church were greeting me as the "old married woman!" I was 23! I was not old and didn't want to be old. I'm sure it all sounds quite comical now, but I assure you it was not at all comical to me at the time. With all of this newness swirling around me and all these ridiculous expectations I put on myself weighing me down, I spent about three months living my daily life but honestly wondering if it would be better if one of us just died and I could get out of this. (Suicide wasn't an option, and neither was divorce, and besides, I adored him!) I was terrified to fail at this marriage, and my fears had become so unreasonable that I was miserable spending my life with this man I passionately loved. Satan had gotten a stronghold of fear into me, and it ruled my life.

The breakthrough moment came for me one Sunday night as I knelt at the altar down front in my father's church. I was crying out to God, trying to get him to give me enough strength to endure this the rest of my life and not mess it up. The Lord said to me very gently, "Nancy, you're so worried about seven years from now that you're not enjoying being his wife now. You just enjoy being Mrs. Shannon Schreyer today, and I'll take care of seven years from now." That was it. That's all it took. I said, "OK." I did have to decide.

I made a decision right then that I was not going to worry anymore (worry is a sin, by the way) and I was going to enjoy getting to be the bride of the most wonderful man in the world. Now here I am over thirty three years later, even more in love and ridiculously blessed and happy with this amazing man! Satan lied to me, and I bought into it and almost lost this precious gift and destiny God had for me. God is for you, and He is for your marriage. He has the answer for any problem or situation; just ask Him.

Our relationship with God is much like our marriage. Its value cannot even be imagined. It must be guarded carefully every day. It's all those little things that we think don't matter that make the difference between a rich, full relationship or a shallow religion that only goes through the motions. Do you treat God the way you would like to be treated? Do you honor Him and treasure Him? Is He your first thought in the morning and your last thought at night? No one means to let their marriage go. We get distracted, take each other for granted. We do the same thing with God. We get caught up in all the "stuff" of life and soon our relationship with Him is on shaky ground. There's such distance between us that we can't hear His voice. The incredible thing about Jesus is that He's always ready to get back together. You never have to wonder if He wants you back. You never have to wonder if He still loves you. You never have to wonder if you'll be able to work it out. The answer is always yes.

How closely are you guarding your marriage? How carefully do you watch all those little things day by day? Don't assume it will just work out. Just like keeping your body in shape takes daily commitment, so does keeping your marriage in shape.

And the same is true of your marriage to Christ. Every day you need to make it a point to keep Him first, spend time with Him, talk to Him, listen to Him. Honor Him and put Him first. Tell other people how in love you are with Him. Get to know Him---I guarantee you that there will always be something new to learn. Let Him love you. Let Him show you how good He is and all the incredible gifts He has for you. Spend a lifetime, then an eternity, in the most passionate, powerful, exhilarating relationship you could ever imagine. It's worth the investment.

CHAPTER 14:
Going Deeper

1. List at least five skills needed to maintain a good marriage.

   _____

   _____

   _____

   _____

   _____

2. One of the biggest mistakes couples make is:

   _____

   _____

   _____

3. If you don't understand the _____ of your marriage, you probably will not guard it well.

4. What's the best general rule for a good marriage (and all our other relationships)?

    _____

    _____

    _____

5. What passages tell us Jesus' attitude about His "rights" ?

    _____

    _____

    _____

6. How did that turn out for Him?

    _____

    _____

    _____

7. What's a good verse when you feel like you just can't stand something anymore?

    _____

    _____

    _____

8. What are the main five "love languages" according to Gary Smalley?
    a. _____
    b. _____
    c. _____
    d. _____
    e. _____

9. What do you think your top two love languages are?
    a. _____
    b. _____

10. What do you think your spouse's top two love languages are?

   a. _____

   b. _____

11. Of the "safeguards" mentioned, what 5 do you most need to work on with your spouse?

   a. _____

   b. _____

   c. _____

   d. _____

   e. _____

12. Of the safeguards mentioned, which five do you need to work on most with God?

   a. _____

   b. _____

   c. _____

   d. _____

   e. _____

"Great goals are achieved by accomplishing small tasks pertaining to them every day. If you do that, you cannot help but reach your goal."
John Maxwell

Your marriage is meant to be a treasure. Take time to invest in it!

Notes / Thoughts / Prayer

_____

_____

_____

_____

_____

Having a marriage that mirrors the relationship that Christ longs for with His bride is not an easy accomplishment. It takes a supernatural love and a lifetime of pouring yourself into another person.

CHAPTER 15:
Divorce and Reconciliation:

"Returning to your first love."

It almost seems "Pollyanna-ish" to write a chapter like this, but I do so because I believe what I write with all my heart. God is the ultimate reconciler. Second Corinthians 5:18 says that God has reconciled us to Himself through Christ and that now we have been given the ministry of reconciliation. He is all about what we perceive as the fairy tale—but for Him it is absolute reality because it is His kingdom and He determines what reality is. For some of us, we live by the old song line, "Wasn't it me who said, 'Nothin' good's gonna last forever?' Wasn't it me who said, 'Let's just be glad for the time together?'" (Diana Ross 1973). But God always has a plan so good that it's beyond our imagination (Ephesians 3:20, Jeremiah 29:11, 1 Corinthians 12:9). God is the perfect romantic! He always longs to see the bride rescued from the evil villain and swept off her feet by her handsome prince, carried to His kingdom of safety that is breathtakingly beautiful, where they live passionately and joyfully ever after! That's God's plan for us, and He has paid the highest price imaginable to make it happen; now it's just up to us to choose that ending.

I carry no illusions about the difficulty and complexity of reconciliation in a human relationship. I've spent far too much time counseling couples who are at the end of their marital rope and are using every bit of self-restraint to keep from tying a noose in that same rope and forcing it over their spouses' heads! To quote again the brilliant (and very wise) words of my husband, "You didn't get in to this problem overnight, and you're not going to get out of it overnight." (That's also a tremendously freeing truth when people call at 3:00 AM and expect you to immediately and completely clean up the pieces of their marital explosion.) Relational dysfunctions are rarely one-sided and stem from root issues of unhealthy beliefs and life patterns from both sides. We live our lives according to what we perceive through the life lenses each of us wear. Many times those lenses are distorted, thus causing us to see things in a distorted manner, but most times we don't even think we have any lenses on, so we swear that what we are seeing is accurate. We make judgments and decisions according to what we think reality is, and as a result, damage our relationships and ourselves. In almost every case we pass those misperceptions on to our children and the cycle of dysfunction and pain just rolls on from generation to generation. All the while we think that the rest of the world is so cruel and messed up, and that nothing good ever really works out, when all we really need is a new set of glasses.

New glasses are formed by new mindsets. The Bible clearly shows us the need for this process. We are forgiven instantly, by grace, which is a gift (Ephesians 2:8,9), but we are "transformed by the renewing of your mind" (Romans 12:2). It goes on to say that when our minds are renewed we are then able to understand what God's will is. Ever felt confused about what God's will is? We need clear lenses in order to have clear perception. We need our minds transformed into the mind of Christ so we can see things as He does; then we can live our lives the way he has designed them to be lived.

The old saying "Sticks and stones may break my bones, but words can never hurt me." is one of the biggest fallacies our parents ever told us. A broken bone will heal in a matter of weeks, while a wounded heart can stay unhealed for a lifetime. There are emotional wounds that occur in relationships that can affect what we think about others and ourselves for the rest of our lives. Our experiences and how we deal with them, good and bad, form our lenses. If those wounds are not healed we live our lives as wounded people. The saying "Hurt people hurt people." is very true. We "leak" what we are. That would all seem hopeless if it were not for the overwhelming power of God's grace that "covers a multitude of sin" (1 Peter 4:8) and gives us "beauty for ashes" (Isaiah 61:3). One thing I have learned over the last several years is " I can control only myself," another amazingly freeing concept. But it's also a frustrating concept when we desperately want to control the decisions other people make and the way those decisions affect our lives. No one can deny the fact that it takes two people to make a relationship work. And a healthy relationship requires two healthy people — quite a rare commodity nowadays.

There's an old saying that the definition of a fool is someone who keeps doing the same thing the same way and yet expects a different result. Some of us think that everyone of the opposite sex is a jerk because we've been in multiple relationships that ended in the same painful way. We've never stopped to consider that the one constant in the equation was us! So how do we heal those wounds, quit living our lives out of old hurts and habits, have our minds transformed into the mind of Christ, and get some new, clear lenses to look through? I think it's important to understand that being transformed is a process. Jesus can come in and remove old lenses like a doctor removes a cataract, but Satan will try to come in and put them back on us, so even if we have a transformative God encounter, we still need to learn to live everyday life wearing our new lenses. Because of years of seeing people and situations through our old lenses, we will be tempted to continue to interpret them the same way we always have. Our natural tendency is to react, not respond, to circumstances. Something or someone triggers an old hurt and we just lash out the only way we know how to protect ourselves. And Satan has no new tricks; he will keep trying what has worked on us in the past until he is convinced that it is now powerless.

The most powerful truth in being transformed is that we become like the one we are with. It is vital that we spend our days in His presence, always abiding in Him. It doesn't mean we don't do anything else but pray; it means we live with a continual awareness that He is with us. We go about our day, think our thoughts, filter our feelings and actions through the knowledge that He is right there beside us, the focus of our lives. We must spend time getting to know Him, how He thinks, what His heart is toward others and us. We need to know what His word says, and know Him personally by spending time with Him. Then His eyes become our eyes, His heart becomes our heart, and His lenses become our lenses. It gives us a whole new way to view our world, our relationships, and circumstances. Then we are able to respond rather than react, and we do so the way He would. We can love the way He loves and forgive the way He forgives. It's a completely different way to live for many of us who grew up in homes where the mind and love of Christ were never considered. It's not an easy process, but it is definitely freeing, empowering, and rewarding. We can't control how anyone else acts or responds, but we can live in control of our own actions and emotions. Although there is no guarantee of a positive response from the other person (remember, each person is in control of himself or herself), the love of Christ is the most powerful force in existence. When we love the way He does, we become nearly irresistible.

Now let's look at some practical rules to live by for loving and responding according to the heart of God:

- I will know Him (through prayer and His word) so that I will know how He would respond before a situation ever occurs. I must know what true love looks like.
- I will set guidelines in place for myself that dictate my behavior no matter what the circumstance. For instance: I will not respond in anger toward anyone and dishonor him or her (yelling, cussing, belittling, etc.).

- I will choose to believe the best and seek to understand the root of the other person's behavior, not just judge the behavior. I will dig for treasure, not dirt, in people's lives.
- I will choose to see others in light of the purpose and destiny God has for them and I will remember that my battle is against spiritual powers, not any person.
- I will manage myself in every relationship, and I will remember that I am not and cannot be responsible for others' behavior, but I am completely responsible for my own.
- I will live my life from the truth that because I have Christ and His love in me, I also have a never-ending supply of love available to those around me. (I can do all things through Christ who strengthens me! Philippians 4:13)
- I have the fruit of the Spirit--love, joy, peace, longsuffering, kindness, goodness, faithfulness, gentleness, self-control--they are all one fruit!
- I have the God-over-the-impossible living in me. He can do all things no matter how hopeless it may seem.
- I will live a supernatural life with my supernatural God.

I think probably the hardest part of restoring a relationship is not holding on to the heartache of the past. Satan loves to bring condemnation on us; he loves to dredge up unforgiveness and hurt. Satan is the complete opposite of love and grace. But if we are going to be able to completely restore any relationship, we have to live by grace. We have to forgive the way we were forgiven---completely, totally, with no debt still owed to us from the one who hurt us. Wow! That's a new way of thinking. "I'm going to make this up to you" or "You're going to pay for this" cannot be any part of the deal. People need to be able to have a fresh start, to move on. It doesn't mean we're foolish about our relationships or how we allow people to treat us, but it does mean that either a debt is forgiven, or not. It can't be a "loan modification," so to speak. It can't be that they still owe you, but can now pay you back under better conditions. That's not forgiveness or grace. Grace can seem really frightening for the person offering it, because it has no strings attached. It is complete. It leaves us vulnerable to being hurt again. It takes a chance that although we may choose to believe the best in someone, he or she may choose to make another bad choice. But that's how God lives life. We mess up, He forgives us and lets us start all over again—clean slate—with no guarantee that we won't turn right around and do the same thing all over again. That's an incredible way to live and rarely risked by humans.

I totally understand that trust has to be rebuilt in a relationship where it has been broken. I understand that a strong, positive balance needs to be built back up in a place that far too many withdrawals have taken place. But with God, we can do that and still give people full forgiveness and a fresh start. It all has to be part of the package, along with new lenses to look at our lives, new skills in communication and honoring one another, and a fresh commitment to each other and the covenant we have made. There was never just one thing that was the problem, and it was never something that just happened overnight.

Having a marriage that mirrors the relationship that Christ longs for with His bride is not an easy accomplishment. It takes a supernatural love and a lifetime of pouring yourself into another person. It takes the fruit of the spirit in full harvest. But it is absolutely possible and absolutely God's will for every marriage. He is God over the impossible. He will do exceedingly abundantly over everything you could ask or even imagine. It's not a task we've been given; rather, it's a gift we've been given, and if we will press into it with all our hearts, it will be the amazing adventure of a lifetime.

Lastly, but most importantly, there are those of us who find ourselves "divorced" from God. Maybe we can identify the event we feel that caused it, or maybe as in so many human relationships, we feel that we just drifted apart from God or "fell out of love" with Him. It makes no difference to Him how it happened. What He longs for us to know is that He is always ready to reconcile. He doesn't struggle to forgive and forget. It takes no effort on His part to love us. He IS love and loves us the same—perfectly—whether our choices have been good or bad, have pleased Him or hurt Him, and whether we love Him or hate Him. A new covenant and a fresh start are always available from Him. He always believes in your destiny with Him, because He is the one who created it! He doesn't have to dig and dig to find treasure in you, because He sees right through your dirt. The Bible says that perfect love casts out all fear (1 John 4:8). There need not be any fear in coming to Him no matter what you have done or how long you have been "divorced" from Him. He loves you deeply and wants to be in a relationship with you. He has given everything to make you His bride. If you have rejected that offer for any reason, He is offering it again right now. He is ever before you with His arms wide open, eyes twinkling, and the biggest smile you've ever seen, asking, "Will you marry me?" Say yes!

CHAPTER 15:
Going Deeper

1.   How do we know that God desires reconciliation?

_____

_____

_____

_____

_____

2.   List three scriptures that show God has a good plan for us.

a. _____

b. _____

c. _____

3.   We are forgiven by _____, but we are transformed by _____.

4.   What forms our "lenses?"

_____

_____

_____

_____

_____

5.   What are some faulty lenses you have looked through in the past or tend to look through now?

_____

_____

_____

_____

_____

6.   "Hurt people _____ people."

7.   What does a healthy relationship require?

_____

_____

_____

_____

_____

_____

8.   Transformation isn't instant, it's a _____.

9.   We will become like the _____.

10.   What are some practical rules to "love" by:

_____

_____

_____
_____
_____
_____

11.   Define forgiveness:

_____
_____
_____
_____
_____

12.   What are some things necessary for reconciliation?

_____
_____
_____
_____
_____

13.   Why do we not need to fear reconciling with God?

_____
_____
_____
_____
_____

Notes / Thoughts / Prayer

_____
_____
_____
_____
_____

CHAPTER 15: DIVORCE & RECONCILIATION

Closing Prayer and Blessing

God, I thank You for all those who have taken the time to read this book. I pray that You would give us a fresh understanding and deeply rooted confidence in Your indescribable love. Let us have a secure, tenacious grasp of Your faithfulness and Your always-good plan for our lives. Uproot any lies Satan has planted in our spirits and deeply anchor Your truth in its place. You are always good, all the time. You have ordained our days before we were even placed in our mothers' wombs. We long to have that intimate relationship of a cherished bride with her faithful lover. We want to know you deeply and passionately. We want to spend our lifetime and eternity being one with You. Let our lives and our relationships reflect our loving, intimate marriage to You. Amen.

Made in the USA
Las Vegas, NV
16 December 2022